PHOENIX

YETTA POWELL

Printed and bound in Great Britain by:
ProPrint,
Riverside Cottages,
Old Great North Road, Stibbington,
Cambridgeshire PE8 6LR

CONTENTS

FOREWORD

These articles and poems were printed and published in 'News & Views' from 1996 to 2004 — a magazine sent to healers in the UK., N America, Israel and S Africa - edited by my husband and myself.

My intention in writing them was to inform, interest and inspire our readers, and I hope these excerpts will do the same for you.

My grateful thanks and appreciation to Shirley Stockman for her great illustrations and to my husband Maurice for his loving support, encouragement and hard work in preparing this book for publication.

'There are two ways to live your life.
One is as though nothing is a miracle, the
other is as though everything is a miracle'

Albert Einstein

'I write poetry because the English word
'inspiration' comes from the Latin 'spiritus' -
breath. I want to breathe freely.'

Alan Ginsberg

DEDICATION

This book is dedicated to all those who send out love, light
and healing, in the hope and belief that peace and
harmony for all beings will one day manifest on this Earth.

TO THE READER

I chose the quotations for this book because they spoke to
my 'heart' as I hope they speak to yours.

THE PHOENIX

The phoenix, although a bird of fable, occurs in Egyptian, Chinese and Islamic mythology and appears on the coinage of the late Roman Empire as a symbol of the Eternal City.

It was said to be as large as an eagle with 'brilliant red and gold plumage and a melodious cry.'

According to fable, only one phoenix existed at one time and lived no less than 500 years, eternally renewing itself in fire. Towards the end of its life, it built a nest of spice branches, set it on fire and was consumed by the flames. From the ashes, a new phoenix would spring forth, so a phoenix always existed.

It is associated with immortality and is an emblem of the sun and resurrection.

I see it as a symbol of hope for the future in a world of turmoil, fear and uncertainty.

* * * *

'I believe in the future, however distant, when no one will go hungry,
there will be no war, no fanaticism, and no conflict between others,
when each nation shall bless each nation and live in peace.'

Maimonides

FLY LIKE A PHOENIX

Wondrous bird of fire
Rise from the ashes
Of despair and desire

Soar to the heights
Of radiance and bliss
Ignore sadness and fear
Yes it can be like this.

Your cage door is open
You can be free
Leave behind the bars
Of negativity

Let joy lift you high
It is your birthright
Peace and love reign supreme
For you - creature of Light!

* * * *

'Faith is the bird that feels the light when the dawn is still dark.'

Tagore

KALI YUGA

We live in a remarkable era. This has been called Kali Yuga, the age of darkness and illusion, the darkest age humanity has yet experienced.

It is a time of much chaos, brutality and intolerance, racial prejudice, greed, hunger for power, lack of respect for human life, animals and other forms of life. It is a time of famine, disease, earthquakes and volcanic eruptions all over the world, massacres and war such as have never been known before.

Every day, the media reports horrific happenings and crimes, innocents suffering unspeakably, and it is as if we are becoming so immune to these horrors, that we hardly raise an eyebrow any more, let alone voice a protest.

And yet there is great hope for there are always some voices to be heard — some great souls — to remind us that we are spiritual beings inhabiting human bodies on this Earth, in order to enjoy the gift of life we have been given so lovingly and kindly - a priceless gift - and to learn at this Earthly School of Life.

To those who have the awareness, every breath is precious, putting us in touch with and recognising the Source of all life and creation, love, peace, light, beauty, energy and truth.

We are so blessed, since this Source of Creation - we call God - doesn't live far, far away 'up in the sky' as it were, but dwells in each human heart with infinite kindness and unconditional love, allowing us all access if we so wish - particularly through prayer and meditation.

We have made incredible strides in technology over the past 50 — 100 years. The past century has been phenomenal in the way such great advances have been made enabling us to communicate globally through computer Internet, to travel further and faster, to speak to and see people thousands of miles away and so on.

We have been given gadgets to relieve us of drudgery, more and more leisure pursuits to enjoy, ways hopefully to improve health and happiness.

But are we any happier?

Fundamentally we all hunger for simplicity, joy and happiness and these are natural bom gifts that we see in little children. They are to be found within us, not in the complicated, constantly beckoning distractions outside. These say 'try this, try that!' 'Buy this and buy that!' but no matter how much we try and buy there is no lasting satisfaction.

For us as healers and knowing others like ourselves, we hopefully have the awareness to recognise the true hunger in the people we meet and give healing to. We understand that we are spiritual beings endeavouring to grow in the process of enlightenment and the purpose of life, which is to accept and realise God and, to leam and enjoy this gift of life.

As healers we can help others to recognise this so that they can be in touch with the peace, joy and love within themselves.

We are truly fortunate for we can now all help the age which has already begun and which has been promised to us, in which darkness and illusion and ignorance and fear are dispelled,

- so that the Golden Age of harmony, joy and peace may prevail
- when 'men shall be brothers,' for even a very little light will dispel darkness.

* * * *

'Some day, after we have mastered the winds, the waves, the tides andgravity, we shall harness the energies of love. Then for the second time in the history of the world, man will havediscovered fire. '

Pierre Teilhard

THE POWER OF THOUGHT

There has been a great deal of writing and information, particularly in the last ten years, about thought, positive thinking, affirmations and so on. Most of us as healers, are aware of the power of thought; that is that thought is a powerful energy which has a profound effect on us and everyone we meet. As Edgar Cayce the American mystic and healer said many years ago, 'We are what we eat and what we think.'

It is known that our thoughts affect our emotions and that our emotions affect the chemical balance of our bodies and minds. Chemical imbalance creates physical and mental discord, discomfort and subsequently dis/ease ... disease.

It seems that many, many people are unaware of this. After all we have millions of thoughts every day, they come fast and furious and uncalled for. Very often we are not even fully conscious of them.

We know that in reality we are truly not our thoughts, and we are not our emotions, and when we are conscious of this, we can, to some extent, control our thoughts rather than allowing them to control and enslave us. The more we become aware of our thoughts, the more this is possible.

As healers, when it is appropriate, we will show a patient how thought affects the body. Constant negative thoughts of hate, anger, sadness, fear, resentment, etc., will weaken the body, while positive thought of joy, happiness, love, contentment, etc., will strengthen it. This can be shown quite simply and clearly in an instant with a muscle test.

This is an eye opener for them and always amazes them. It's not magic, just simple common sense.

Our thoughts affect us and make us the kind of people we are. It is worthwhile trying to watch our thoughts and make them as habitually positive as possible.

Every action, idea, discovery, work of art, poem, etc., is preceded by a thought.

It is not only what we think and think about that affects us, but indeed everything in our environment. Our world can inspire and uplift us, or depress and pollute us.

Beautiful music, paintings, poems, works of art, natural surroundings (trees, flowers, birds, animals, etc) can make us feel so good, for they are being responded to by the beauty, peace, love and appreciation within our heart and soul. Conversely, harsh music, crude art, sick poetry and literature, TV, and an ugly environment, can definitely pollute us. It is said that the Arts reflect the society in which we live, and it is obvious that we live at present in a sick, impoverished and polluted society. So it is up to us. We have the will. We can choose what we think, see and hear etc., to some extent. We can allow beauty and love and goodness to enrich us or the reverse.

We, as healers, all know how powerful and profound absent or distant healing is, and we can all choose to heal, with our thoughts, other human beings and ourselves; indeed in so doing, the planet Earth itself. We can send out thoughts of gratitude for our lives and all we are given, and transmit thoughts of love and light and peace every day.

FOOD FOR THOUGHT

If I don't control my mind,
My mind controls me,
And will fill me full
Of negativity.

After all, who wants to feel
Depressed, sad and awful,
When you can choose to be
Happy, glad and cheerful.

In France, in the 17th century lived
A philosopher, a very wise man
Called Rene Descartes, who said we're told
'I think, therefore I am!'

The answer to his existence
Is what it seems he sought
But the truth is that what we are right now
Is what we have ever thought.

CELEBRATION

Join in the celebration.
Enjoy the beauty,
And experience the joy,
And appreciate the gift,
Of this precious thing
Called Life!

Join in the
celebration, Dance
with the music, And
sing to the melody,
And sway to the
rhythm Of this
precious gift Called
Life!

Join in the celebration,
See the shining colours,
And the light and the glory,
And the radiant rainbow,
Of this precious gift.
Called Life!

Join in the celebration,
Breathe in the perfume,
And taste the sweetness,
Be here and now,
In this precious gift
Called Life!

* * * *

*'The same stream of life that runs through my veins night and
day, runs through the world, and dances in rhythmic
measures. It is the same life that shoots in joy through the
dust of the Earth in numberless blades of grass and breaks
into tumultuous waves of leaves and flowers. '*

Rabindranath Tagore

THE HEALING POWER OF MUSIC ...

'If music be the food of love play on'...
'The man who has music in his soul..

Music in all its forms is one of our greatest gifts, the healing power of music is incredible - as a tonic to uplift us, soothing sounds to relax us, stirring music to excite us and so on.

Every culture and race has its music - its rhythm, its melodies, its dances and its songs from Africa to South America, from Italy to India - all have their own way of expression through music. The diversity is amazing. We all have our own particular likes and favourites, *whether* modem pop music, opera, classical and so on.

It is an individual thing. Some music stays with us and remains our friend throughout our lives or sometimes we discover new songs, new music. And our taste can change through different age.

For me I love the music of Mozart - the sweetness, clarity and melody of it. I never get tired of his 'Clarinet Concerto', or the 'Magic Flute' for example. Johann Strauss waltzes always make me want to waltz round the room and South American music has an effect too.

A few years ago through meeting Joseph Pilbery a well known Conductor and his wife Mary Pilbery, an equally well known solo oboist, I got to know the concert orchestra that they founded, the internationally famous Vivaldi Concertante Orchestra, and through its wonderful concerts I discovered Vivaldi, who wrote an incredible amount of all kinds of music for every instrument, despite suffering from chronic poor health. Everyone of course knows the 'Four Seasons' by Vivaldi, but few appreciate that he wrote more than six hundred other major works and that J S Bach remarked that he owed much of his genius to Vivaldi. I never tire of listening to Vivaldi and can understand how his need to create music enabled him to cope with his ill health.

Maurice is now Chairman of the Vivaldi Concertante Orchestra, and if possible we attend all the concerts they give. Recently there was a glorious concert at the Rose Gardens, St

Albans culminating in a Laser and Firework display, attended by over 2500 concert goers.

Some years ago we met a doctor (medical) who had invented a machine that healed through sound. He maintained that every human being has his or her own sound pattern — wave form
- quite unique to them. It is when the sound pattern goes out of synch or balance that we become ill and vice versa. With his machine he can rebalance the sound waves of a person needing healing. He showed us the results of such re-balancing, with a lady who had a stiff neck and frozen shoulder.

I found it extremely interesting, especially when he said that we hear music not only with our ears but with every cell in our bodies. In much the same way Electro Crystal healing uses crystal frequency vibrations to adjust the body. Every cell responds to music and sounds and each part accepts what it needs or likes, and rejects the rest. This was all new to me. But let us think of sounds we like and those we don't and their effect - a cat's purr, a road drill, a baby's gurgles, a child's scream, a blackbird's song, a noisy radio.

Our world today is so full of sounds that we don't want to hear. It's very seldom that there is real silence, real peace, real stillness. We can't shut down our ears, as we can close our eyes, as we are assaulted by noise on all sides.

But there are many beautiful sounds, the sounds of nature
— birds, leaves and trees in the breeze, the buzzing of bees, doves cooing etc. Music of the great composers is clearly inspired to fill us full of wonder and joy.

* * * *
'We are members of a vast cosmic orchestra in which each living instrument is essential to the complementary and harmonious playing of the whole. '
L Allen Boone

HEALING

I feel gratitude and awe,
That I am trusted to heal,
And to listen to others,
And hear how they feel.

Inside each is a little child,
A vulnerable being,
When the healing channels through me,
Their true nature I'm seeing.

I see that everyone is filled with love,
Though perhaps they don't yet know,
Until they experience through healing
That this really is so.

* * * *

'Healing is the restoring of harmony to the living whole. '

Sir George Trevelyan

* * * *

'Grandfather
Sacred One
Teach us love, compassion and honour
That we may heal the Earth
And heal each other. '

An Ojibway Indian Prayer

HELPFUL HERB

Have you heard of St John's Wort? Its Latin name is Hypericum Perforatum. Apparently it's becoming more popular and well known as a help for people suffering from depression and anxiety.

It's been called the sunshine herb because of its power to lift the spirit.

I have recently seen two articles about its beneficial effects and I have tried it myself.

There have been a great many clinical trials of Hypericum extract in Germany where they concluded that it performs as well as Prozac, but without the side effects, and it now outsells Prozac.

In one article I read of a woman of 38 who had been prescribed an anti-depressant by her doctor due to her suffering from depression, panic attacks, palpitations and sleeplessness. She wasn't very keen on taking anti-depressants, so when she heard about the beneficial effects of St John's Wort she started taking it (while at the same time gradually reducing her antidepressant intake).

Apparently it kept her on an even keel and she 'felt great' eventually.

Dr David Wheatley, a psychiatrist, set up a clinical study of St John's Wort (Hypericum Perforatum). Although at first sceptical, he was surprised at the results.

He found that it was as effective as amitriptyline (but without the side effects) and that it acted as an anti-depressant enabling the brain to produce more neurotransmitters, and that it acts on the serotonin and noradrenaline - hormones that affect the mind. Dr Wheatley now uses St John's Wort to treat mild to moderate depression.

According to Dr Wheatley it needs to be taken for about six months to maintain its effect and takes two to three weeks to work, but of course it is always best to consult your doctor first and ask his opinion before taking any drug. Likewise we must remind our patients that we do not diagnose, or prescribe drugs, or in any way sanction that they modify the taking of medically prescribed doses without prior consultation and confirmation of their so doing by their own doctor.

'Before you can cure a man's body, you must cure his mind and before that his soul. '

Plato

* * * *

*'The doctor of the future will give no medicine, but will interest his
patient in the care of the human frame, diet, and the cause and
prevention of disease'*

Thomas Edison

* * * *

*'A wise man ought to realise that health is his most valuable possession
and learn how to treat his illnesses by his own judgement. '*

Hippocrates

WHY?

Why was I bom?
Why am I here?
What must I do?
What is my destiny?

The face looks up
Wide eyes questioningly with trust
So many questions
So many choices
So many roads
So many 'shoulds' or 'must'.

Little one - it's so simple
The answers are within you
You were bom to love
To learn, to help, to know
To grow, to be and to enjoy
Love is your destiny.

*'You live that you may learn to love. You love that you may
learn to live.
No other lesson is required of you.'*

Miradad

* * * *

'To love and be loved, this on Earth is the highest bliss.'

Heinrich Heine

* * * *

'Everything in life is holy.'

**Neale Donald Walsch from
'Conversation with God**[9]

13

GETTING OVER DEPRESSION AND RELIEVING STRESS

1. Suggest that they try to be with happy, positive people not those who drain them.

2. Encourage them to watch funny films and videos.

3. Let them be tested for allergies and intolerances to food etc., e.g. a wheat allergy can make you feel depressed. (Body and Mind are connected and affect each other).

4. They might try massage, aromatherapy, reflexology, these are healing too.

5. Remind them to give and receive lots of hugs. Touch is important.

6. Encourage some exercise - walking is very good, especially walking amongst trees, or flowers, or near flowing water etc. Doing so is very tranquillising. Yoga is good, also swimming.

7. Have them write down how they feel (they can always tear it up). Writing poetry is a wonderful therapy for depression too. And remember, it doesn't have to rhyme.

8. Suggest they listen to beautiful music (even if it makes them cry). It will enrich them. Reading good light books not rubbish, also fights depression.

9. Looking at beautiful works of art and craft, trying to paint or make something for themselves, or for others to enjoy, is excellent therapy. Playing around with paint, clay, etc., knitting, embroidering, or just doing anything they enjoy.

10. Encourage them to stroke an animal - a cat or dog and tell them to speak to them about how they feel. It can be very healing. Remind them that animals never judge or criticise you. They just let you hold a paw!

11. Eating properly - *Not junk food* - salads, fruit, lots of vegetables. Suggest cutting out as much as possible, chocolates, coffee, sugar, fried foods.

12. Teach them to breathe properly - deeply from the abdomen.

13. Have them close their eyes and focus on their breath for five minutes - it's very, very calming.

14. If possible put on some music and move to it - dance! Try it to a lively Strauss waltz.

15. Encourage them to pamper themselves - lavender oil in their bath, some new lipstick, etc., a new dress or hair do, or new tie etc.

    Remind them that they are important!
    That they are special!

16. Have them write down all the good things in their life no matter how small. They will be amazed how many there are — have them thank God for them. Gratitude is very uplifting and floods the heart with love - it opens it up and takes away depression.

17. Get them to hug themselves and to rock themselves like a baby. Have them put their hands over their solar plexus and breathe into that area slowly and gently.

18. Have them write and read the affirmations that you follow.
    - Over and over again.

19. Have them write down and keep a book of quotes that inspire them. (It's good for healers to keep such a book too). Write them down.

20. Get them to place a photo of themselves where they will see it many times a day, one that shows them smiling and happy, which will encourage them to see themselves as that again. Or have them visualise themselves happy and smiling.

21. See that they have the right supplements and vitamins to keep them healthy. Suggest trying the Dr Bach flower remedies.

22. Tell them to be sure to get enough rest and sleep - not to allow themselves to get too tired (or too hungry or too cold).

23. Finally - *Tell them to let go of the past. Not to worry about the future — to live for now and let enjoyment flow into their lives.*

AFFIRMATIONS

1. I deserve to enjoy good health.
2. Every moment that passes, I am feeling stronger and more alive.
3. The world is a loving place and I am at home here.
4. I see with loving eyes everyone and everything about me.
5. I can relax into life and trust that it loves me.
6. I drop the past and trust the future will bring me all I need.
7. I let go of the old and welcome the new.
8. Life is fun. I live my life sincerely but without seriousness.
9. I have the courage to stand up for myself.
10. I enjoy my sexuality and my manliness/ womanliness.
11. Iam overflowing with peace, joy and love.
12. It is OK to take time and space to do what I want todo.
13. There is no need to rush, I have always been here and I shall always be here.
14. There is no need to feel guilt. Everything happens as it should.
15. I love and accept myself totally, just as I am right now.
16. Iam totally loveable just for being who I am.
17. I am completely free to create my life as I choose.
18. I can express myself freely and with confidence.
19. I express my love and creativity in my work.
20. I respect myself just for being who I am.
21. I forgive with all my heart everyone who has ever hurt me and wish them well.
22. Nobody has power over me, I am totally free.
23. I am grateful for being alive, and enjoy myself more each day.
24. The world is an abundant place and I deserve to be prosperous.
25. *It really is OK for me to have a good time.*

THESE THINGS ARE FREE

These things are free -
The sparkling stars,
The sky above,
The dewy grass,
Friendship and love
Mountains, lakes, rivers,
Sunsets, moonshine,
The dawn, the morning air
Sweeter than wine.
The air, the water,
Autumnal trees,
Sweet smelling roses
Butterflies, honey bees.
The storm, the rainbow,
Refreshing sleep,
The song of birds,
A memory to keep.
The hoot of owls,
The dove's sweet coo,
Incredible free gifts from God,
For me and for you.
The smiles, the laughter,
The tears that sometimes flow.
The voice within that whispers,
'My child, I know, I know.'

* * * *

'Every person's life is a fairy tale written by God's fingers.
'

Hans Christian Anderson

PEACE

I see peace in the tiny baby fast asleep.
Peace in the sheep grazing quietly on the hill.
Peace in the silvery moonlight softly shining down,
As by the weeping willow I stand still.
Peace in the murmuring stream flowing thru the
fields.
Peace in the sweet, fresh, fragrant early morn.
Peace in the diamond dew that sparkles on the grass.
Peace in each pure creature newly born.
Peace in the soft, gentle doves cooing overhead.
Peace in the bright eyed blackbird singing in the tree.
The peace we experience in this world.
Reflects the true peace within you, within me.
May this true peace within us
Given at birth
Manifest soon
In everlasting peace on earth.

* * * *

I am the Light, I am Love
I am Goodwill and I am Peace
And through me will flow the great energy
That will pour out to all the Earth
and to all the people on the Earth
that will bring Peace, Love and Goodwill
To all on Earth. '

Messages of Light, Israel

TRUTH

When the Lord decided to create the universe, he created the seas, the mountains, the flowers and the clouds. Then He created human beings. Finally He created Truth.

At this point however a problem arose: where should He hide Truth so that humans would not find it right away? He wanted to prolong the adventure of the search.

So the Lord asked his angels.

'Let's put Truth on top of the highest mountain,' said one of the angels 'Certainly it will be hard to find there.'

'Let's put it on the furthest star,' said another angel.

'Let's hide it in the darkest and deepest abyss,' said
another.

'Let's conceal it on the secret side of the moon,' another suggested.

Finally the Lord said 'No we will hide truth inside the very heart of human beings. In this way they will look for it all over the universe without being aware of having it inside themselves all the time.'

* * * *

'No more words. Hear only the voice within. '

Rumi

* * * *

*Not knowing how near Truth is, people seek it far away - what a pity. They are like him, who in the midst of water cries in thirst imploringly. '

Harvin

INSPIRATION

We invite readers of 'News & Views' to send in an article on someone who has inspired them and whom you admire and appreciate. It can be a person alive or dead who is considered famous, or maybe someone only you know, perhaps a friend, relative, parent or healer. So I am going to 'kick off' as it were with someone I have found inspiring ever since I discovered his poems and paintings many years ago and read about his life - *William Blake.*

Although not a spiritual healer, he was a healer in every sense of the word as is shown by his life and work.

William Blake, poet, artist, engraver and painter, mystic and visionary prophet, was bom in London in 1757 into a world that in his time would be mostly unaware of his genius and his work. Apart from a few fellow artists and poets, he was considered 'mad' or at best unworldly, since his views were so unconventional. Those who knew him saw a simplicity, an honesty and a nobility of spirit. He became a master engraver and he and his wife lived modestly, often on the verge of dire poverty. They had no children. William Blake's poems speak to the heart and have a great intensity of feeling. Who has not been stirred by the words of what we now call 'Jerusalem'.

I shall not cease from mental fight
Nor shall my sword sleep in my hand
Till we have built Jerusalem
In England's green and pleasant land.'

Blake wrote of man's enslavement by the laws and rules of society, and of the suffering caused by the Industrial Revolution. He felt that the machinery of industry had reduced man to the level of an unthinking animal, and that it was motivated by greed and economic gain. He wrote compassionately of the misery of his time, the boys who were sent up chimneys to clean them, the dire poverty and hopelessness of the poor, and the uncaring hypocrisy of his time. Walking the London streets he saw *'The marks of woe in every face'* and protested at the social evils and injustices that oppressed every man.

With his prophetic vision he foresaw the state of our modem society, He was opposed to anything which took away man's individuality and freedom. But he felt that change could only come about if men changed themselves, not external circumstances, and raised themselves *'from the deadly sleep of unconsciousness'* so that they could see and perceive reality as it really was. As a mystic he saw angels everywhere, and when his brother died, he wrote that he saw him rising up to heaven, clapping his hands with joy. Blake's prolific output of poetry and prose was self published, because during his lifetime there was no recognition of his outstanding genius. His best known and loved works are *'The Songs of Innocence'* and *'The Songs of Experience'*. Each song has an engraving, created, printed and coloured by Blake himself, helped by his wife. He devised his own unique method of etching both poem and design on a copper plate. He intended in these songs to show *'the two contrary states of the human soul'*. *'Without contraries is no progression. Attraction and Repulsion, Reason and Energy, Love and Hate are necessary to Human Existence'*.

'The Songs of Innocence' have a purity, joy and simplicity. *'The Songs of Experience'* depict how the state of innocence has been converted and perverted by events happening without, and by emotions within.

From Blake's Auguries of Innocence:

'To see a World in a Grain of Sand

And Heaven in a Wild Flower,

Hold Infinity in the palm of your hand,

And Eternity in an hour. '

From Blake's Songs of Innocence:

Infant Joy
I have no name
I am but two days old -
What shall I call thee?
Joy is my name,-
Sweet Joy befall thee!

Pretty joy!
Sweet Joy but two days old.
Sweet joy I call thee:
Thou dost smile.
I sing the
while
Sweet joy
befall thee.

Blake died in 1827, poor and neglected and was buried in an unmarked grave. It was not until 1863 that his work became known and in 1927 his centenary was commemorated, and his work brought his genius to the full attention of the 20th century. He has been called 'the herald of the new age'. So much more could be written about Blake, but do read his poems, and see his paintings at the Tate Gallery. They will inspire you too.

* * * *

'When the doors of perception are cleansed, then all
things will appear
as they truly are - infinite. '

William
Blake

* * * *

'In the gentle relief of another's care
In the darkness of night and the winter's snow
In the naked and outcast
Seek love there.'

William
Blake

I AM CAT

In response to an article by dog which appeared in a recent issue of News & Views, I, Chico the Chinchilla cat thought I would write a more *dignified* version of what it means to be a cat (a much more superior species; I'm sure you will all agree.

After all we are cleaner, much more attractive, don't need to go for walks and we are now more popular than dogs!

Yes *I know* that I am beautiful
As I recline upon your chair
Yes *I know* that you adore me
Yes I do know that you care

You may comb my silky fur
If you really do so wish
As long as when you've finished
You put fish in my dish

You may stroke me very gently
That for you, I will allow
But when I feel I've had enough
You will hear a loud 'miaow!'

You may admire my emerald eyes
And wonder at my feline grace
And I may well decide and deign to
Lick your hand and perhaps your face
When I am contented
You will hear me purr
You may put out your hand
And touch my gorgeous fur.

If you are very good
I may sleep on your bed

Either sometimes at your feet
Or on the pillow above your head.

Then in the dark hours before dawn
I'll wake you with 'miaow! Miaow!'
To tell you that I want out
And I want to go out now!

I *can* go in and out from my cat flap
Which is by the back door mat
But I really prefer *you* to open the door
For after all **I AM CAT**!

(As dictated to my willing and devoted slave Yetta).

CATS

Cats can ignore you
Or may choose to adore you
Cats can irritate
Or your worries eliminate

Cats are never fidgety,
And keep their dignity,
They have a certain charm
And never cause alarm.

DOLPHINS!

 Sitting in the sunshine in March by the Red Sea watching those delightful dolphins swimming and cavorting and leaping out of the water at Dolphin Reef was idyllic. Ships passed by and Aquaba in Jordan across the water seemed so near, and it was so peaceful, due, I am sure to the presence of those divine creatures.

We had been fortunate enough to be able to have a week in Eilat, my birthday treat.

Enjoying it all, I was struck by the contrast of peace and tranquillity here with the dolphins, and the tension and threat of war in Israel.

Speaking to a healer from Germany who was primarily there to observe the dolphins, who she said can teach us all so much - humour, healing, playfulness and joy of living - she remarked, 'Well they don't have minds to worry them as we do.'

Then I began to think about all of us.

Here we are wanting to be happy and peaceful and enjoy this gift of life as we are meant to do. Yet we have this mind, this 'chattering monkey' that seems to sit on our shoulder, constantly and incessantly telling us what to do, to do this and that, try this and that, keeping us full of fear and guilt. It can drive us crazy.

I'm not saying that we don't need to think. Of course we do, but we can try to be positive and be master of our thoughts, not the slave. We do need our brains and we do need to think.

Yet there is another part of us - call it the heart (not the physical heart) where we can feel peace and love and joy despite whatever is going on. Meditation can take us to that place of deep inner peace which is our true home.

When we remember the story of Moses coming down from the mountain with the Ten Commandments and finding the children of Israel worshipping the Golden Calf, we see how the mind can take control.

Here were the children of Israel whom the Lord God had saved from bondage and had allowed Moses to lead them out of Egypt, forgetting their faith in God, and their true hearts, and allowing their minds to get the better of them. Surely each human being has this challenge between light, peace and good versus darkness, war and evil. The fight is within, not outside: It is a life long battle each must win. Shalom - Peace.

* * * *

Really I say that the true pilgrimage
is within our heart
One should go there and look
If you have to listen to any voice
Listen to the voice of the heart
If you have to listen to any call
Listen to the call of the heart. '

Maharaji

* * * *

'This life is a gift
It is a priceless gift
It is an incredible gift
We are all so fortunate.'

Maharaji

* * * *

'Nothing happens to you or through you
that is not for your highest good.'

Neale Donald Walsh
From 'Conversations with
God'

SNOW MAGIC

While I slept, the world was transformed
From colour to black and white.
Whiteness, dazzling, glistening
Immobilising the living trees.
Not a leaf moved not a branch swayed.
The oak tree, like Lot's wife
Stood petrified
With icicles and icy tears.

The weeping willow, like a radiant bride,
Spread wide her skirts
Of delicate filigree.
And - all was muffled.

It was a magical land
Strange, dreamlike and mystical,
Quiet, and slow and still,
As if waiting ... waiting ...

And then - a blackbird sang!
A robin flew on to a twig
With breast of blood red brightness
Chirping his sweet, sharp song.

The sun beamed out,
And all glimmered in his light.
The fir tree slipped her lacy cover,
And showed her dark green cloak.

In the sky, a little blue comer showed
And fluffy clouds, pink and grey and white.
The muffled sound of shovels, brooms and
spades
Clear children's voices on their way to
school.

The milkman jangled his bottles
The sound shattering the still air.
It was clear and bright and gay
A feeling of excitement and expectancy.

TOMORROW'S HOPE

The children of today
Are God's gift for tomorrow
Through them a Golden Age of Love
And Joy, will banish sorrow.

They herald a time of peace and hope
And light for all to see
It is not an empty dream
But what is meant to be.

A true brotherhood of man
Will manifest on this Earth
And no child will suffer hunger
Because of humble birth.

All races, religions and nations,
Will live in true harmony
With respect and love for all of life
God's plan for humanity.

* * * *

'I want us to dream God's dream that there will be peace and harmony, and the world's children can live happily and enjoy their childhood.'

Desmond Tutu

HEALING POWER OF GEMSTONES AND CRYSTALS

Gemstones and crystals are treasured for their beauty, rarity and durability, and are considered to have healing properties.

The stone may be held, worn, carried or placed in one's environment. Here are some of them.

Aquamarine

(From aqua marine — Latin for 'sea water'. Coloured bluey green, or green or blue).

It was the eighth foundation stone in the wall of the New Jerusalem. It was used to guard against injury during battle, known as the 'Serene One' and said to calm nerves and reduce fluid retention. It enhances clarity of mind and creative self expression and tolerance. Useful in the treatment of eyesight problems, swollen glands, liver trouble and toothache.

Lapis Lazuli

From the Arabic 'lazaward' = Azure.

Revered as a royal stone in ancient Egypt. In Jewish History, it was probably the 'sapphire on the high priests' breast plate.

It is said to promote friendship and goodwill, and enhance wisdom, inner vision and mental clarity. Known as the stone of truth and integrity it can help to overcome depression and enhance feelings of sincerity and self acceptance and success in friendships.

It is used in disorders of the throat, bone marrow, thymus and the immune system, and can help to relieve insomnia and dizziness.

Sapphire

Rich, deep blue. It is said to be the 'stone of kings' worn to protect them against harm and used in the breast plate of the ancient high priest.

Sapphire is said to help free one of unwanted thoughts, bringing joy and peace of mind, making one more receptive to beauty and intuition. It has been used in the treatment of blood disorders, combating excessive bleeding and strengthening the walls of veins, the relief of insomnia and nervousness.

Turquoise

Pale blue, greenish blue or pale green opaque.

North American Indians valued it as a protective stone and a bestower of goodness and bringer of rain. It is considered by many to be a master healer, helping in the absorption of nutrients, strengthening the entire anatomy and stimulating tissue regeneration. It is particularly good for the throat and lungs, and because of its high copper content is a conductor of healing and good for rheumatism and arthritis. It is believed to enhance creative expression, peace of mind, communication, friendship and loyalty.

* * * *

'The gems cannot be polished without friction, nor man perfected without trials.'

Confucius

* * * *

'Do you imagine the universe is agitated? Go into the desert at night and look at the stars. This practice should answer the question.

Lao Tzu

ON BECOMING A GRANDMOTHER
(To all grandparents or grandparents to be)

I have always been interested in and enjoyed my friends' grandchildren, not having any of my own.

And I was always a little amused at the way they would bring out photographs and dwell on the perfection, intelligence and personality of their own very special grandchild or grandchildren.

Now that we have a beautiful little granddaughter of our own, I fully understand the feeling of those doting besotted grandmas and grandpas, because I am demonstrating the same traits. I too bring out the photos and describe each little development to any captive audience I can find.

Rachael Louise was bom on March 30th 1998 the day after my birthday and when we first saw her at a few hours old, we immediately fell deeply, in love with her — so tiny, so perfect, such exquisite hands and feet.

That love has grown as she has grown. We marvel at this little miracle of life, so pure, so innocent, smiling at everyone and expressing love and joy so easily. It really touches our hearts.

Of course babies are being bom all the time, you may say. It is commonplace. Yet each one is a miracle, each human being so unique. There never was a human being just like you (even if you are twins) and there never will be again.

We are all miracles and we were all babies once, freely expressing joy and love and wonder. Actually in our hearts we are still like small children and we can feel the joy, love, peace and wonder within us if we so wish.

Maybe it needs contact with a newborn baby to remind us of this, and of how precious and priceless is this gift of life, and the gift of living breath that we are given at birth.

There is a quotation which says - 'God shows us every time a child is bom, that He still has faith in human beings.'

When I see a newborn baby or a sleeping baby or child, I am reminded of William Wordsworth's poem when he sees the newborn child 'trailing clouds of glory' from whence he came.

We are enjoying every little development of Rachael's - discovering her fingers, turning over and trying out different sounds, vigorously kicking and lifting her head etc. She converses with us in her own sweet way.

This marvellous drive we see in a baby's rapid development is present in every human being whatever age they may be. As fully grown adults we can no longer grow physically but on other levels - mental, emotional, and especially spiritual, there is a constant need, a thirst to know, to learn, to improve and to love.

* * * *

'Each newborn child brings the message that God has not lost His trust in man.'

Tagore

* * * *

'When you have a grandchild, it is as if a door opens wide in your heart that you never knew was there, and the love just pours out and never stops.'

**Philippa
Lewis**

THIS HOUSE

This house
Once filled with noise
And children and laughter
Reawakens to you -
Rachael
With your joy and your smile
Your sense of fun
Your constant activity
And your first words and sounds.

So You Would Like To Be A Healer

That wonderful healer Harry Edwards called healers the 'salt of the earth . It is said that it is one of the highest things a human being can do. It really is a great privilege to be used as a channel for the healing energies that come from The Source of all energy. We need to realise this and be grateful for the opportunity that has been given to us and the fact that in our hearts we have felt the desire to be healers. It is a commitment, but very rewarding and brings a quiet joy. Fundamentally healing is loving and caring for other human beings in need. There really are healers in every sphere everywhere doing their work, whatever it is, with love. We have to be aware that we are only channels; the healing does not come from us but through us, so we must be humble enough to recognise this and not get into an 'ego trip'. Whether someone gets better or not is not up to us, although it is very gratifying to have helped someone. * Healing is not only concerned with the body, but also the mind, emotions and spirit. It is holistic healing, healing of the whole being. So healing addresses the cause not just the symptoms, and the cause may not necessarily be physical. It can make the person receiving healing realise that they are a spiritual being. We take healing seriously, but we don't have to be too serious or solemn about it. Humour and laughter is very healing, and after all, who created humour and laughter in the first place? It can help to relax the person having healing, who may see the healer as an 'authority' figure, especially if it is their first experience, so put them at their ease. After all we are all human beings doing our best, learning from everything and everyone; the learning process never stops. Don't worry if you feel inadequate or have to say 'I don't know.' It takes strength to say that, and really everyone is in the same boat. Gradually your confidence and trust will increase. Be kind and gentle and take time to listen to everyone, to other healers and people you give healing to. Remember there are many people and books that will help you, but the best helper is your own heart. If you listen to that you can't go wrong. Finally be grateful for the gifts you have been given your life, your breath and healing.

Healing is as simple and natural as breathing, yet so profound.

Basically we are all healers, but as well as a sincere desire to heal, we need as with everything some training to be truly affective.

LITTLE ONE

To a newborn grandchild

Little one,
Precious one,
Child of my child,
Welcome to this Earth.

You have come
'Trailing clouds of glory'
With innocence and joy
Wonder, love and purity.

Little miracle
Blissfully asleep
What potential is there
In that tiny form?

Little hands
So perfect
What will they do
As you grow?

Such sweetness
Such perfection
My heart sings
As I look at you.

As I hold you
In my arms
I feel such joy
And such fulfilment.

You have come
To adorn the world
To heal and to love
And to bring happiness.

MUSIC WASHES AWAY FROM THE SOUL THE DUST OF EVERYDAY LIFE

'The power of music to integrate and cure... is quite fundamental

Averbach.

It is the profoundest non chemical medication. ' Oliver Sacks

Music has a wonderful power to heal; to uplift the heart, to soothe the soul, and to energise or relax the body. It has a great effect on our emotions for surely the great classical music that we hear was divinely inspired.

I'm sure all healers would find a book I've been reading of great interest and benefit: 'The Mozart Effect' - by Don Campbell, published by Hodder and Stoughton - 'tapping the Power of Music to heal the body, strengthen the mind, and unlock the creative spirit.' The latter part of the book is devoted to 'miracle stories of treatment and cure' in which music of all kinds was used to help and heal people with all kinds of illnesses, ailments and disease. It's fascinating reading.

'Each illness has a musical solution, the shorter and more complete the solution, the greater the musical talent of the physician. '

Novalis

It is said that we each have our own unique vibration or sound which when we are well is in harmony, but we can become distressed, ill or diseased when it goes out of synch. Also we hear not only with our ears but with every cell in our body which accepts only those notes it needs and rejects the rest.

We are very privileged to have as a dear friend, a renowned orchestral conductor - Joseph Pilberry, who, with his wife, Mary, a professional oboe player (who is also multi-talented and a gifted artist) has given much pleasure to tens of thousands of people in the UK, Italy, Israel, Switzerland, the Ukraine and USA and on the Orient Express. Here is someone who lives and breathes music and is devoted to it.

Joseph has been conducting for over 50 years at halls such as the Barbican, St John's, St Martins-in-the-Fields, The Festival Hall, etc. He conducts the Vivaldi Concertante and the Millennium Youth Orchestra and has given so many opportunities to young musicians starting on their professional career, many of whom are now concert soloists, and are internationally famous.

We are fortunate to attend many of his concerts since Maurice is Chairman of the Orchestra. We particularly cherish hearing Mozart's Requiem at St Martins, the Verdi Requiem at the Italian Church in Clerkenwell which was an extremely moving experience. Incidentally Mozart is my favourite composer and I positively love his Clarinet Concerto (which we played to our granddaughter Rachael when she was just three hours old. And she smiled! Truly!).

One concert which is most delightful is the annual open air concert held at The Garden of The Rose, St Albans - a Last Night of The Proms event which takes place in August with 23000 concert goers picnicking in these famous gardens before the performance begins and enjoying 'Rule Britannia', 'Land of 'Hope and Glory' and 'Jerusalem' with a programme of good classical music, followed by fireworks and laser display.

Joseph Pilberry was bom in 1931 to Jewish parents living first in Dalston, then Stoke Newington. They were not well off, his father was a furrier, his mother a dressmaker.

There were no musicians in the family and really this is a story of Joseph's love of, or destiny, to devote himself to music and his courageous overcoming of all adversity and obstacles to that end (including poverty).

When Joseph was about 13 he was taken to a concert at the Camden Theatre by a cousin and there his musical destiny began. He has told us how he acquired his first violin. It belonged to a friend - Joseph wanted it so much that his mother gave his suit to the friend in exchange for the violin. And so it began with Joseph practising eight hours a day.

His first lessons were from a 'sweet old lady' in Earls Court who charged l/6d an hour and included real cream cakes and tea!

He studied with other teachers including Tom Jenkins, of the Palm Court Orchestra, who allowed him to play on his Stradivarius. During this time Joseph supported himself by getting a job, in a music shop, selling sheet music.

His first debut as a conductor was conducting the National Anthem at the end of a West End musical. Six years later he was conducting 'The Mikado' with his own orchestra.

When he was 23 he was asked to form an orchestra and conduct for the Albert Hall Festival. Of that momentous event he writes 'I can still see my father crying with happiness.' In 1962 he formed the New World Symphony Orchestra which was jointly conducted by Joseph and Sir Adrian Boult. Later came the New Westminster Philharmonic Orchestra - it was with this orchestra that he became one of that rare breed of conductors who have successfully conducted all the Mahler Symphonies. There is sadly not enough space to write of all Joseph's work and accomplished career. He has conducted in many synagogues and at the Chief Rabbi's home (not the present one) as well as in many halls and churches.

Joseph has always had to struggle to find sponsors since concerts demand a great deal of money. Unfortunately in this day and age, unlike the time of Bach or Beethoven or Mozart, there are no wealthy patrons to support musicians and even the Arts Council is far from forthcoming.

He has learned a great deal about life from the great composers - he has a wealth of information and interest about them. He has said that in order to succeed as a musician one needs talent and training, but also courage, determination and a complete belief in one's destiny. This, Joseph has to a marked degree and is to be greatly admired for this. Also for the joy, happiness and for the healing that his music making has brought to countless numbers over the past fifty years of dedication.

'Music sets up a certain vibration which unquestionably results in a physical reaction. Eventually the proper vibration will be found and utilised. '
George Gershwin

NUTRITION

The words of Hippocrates echo down through the ages and are as true today as they were in 390AD when he wrote them ...

... *'Let food be your medicine, and medicine your food. '*

Over the past five years I have become more and more interested in nutrition and its effect on health. As Edgar Cayce said 'We are what we eat and what we think.' (More about the words of Hippocrates, Cayce and many, many others, who point out the vital part that nutrition has on our well being later). As a healer I believe it is important that we should be aware of factors which can result in poor health and disease and certainly nutrition is one such factor, even though it is not yet universally recognised that this is so. We would not dream of putting inferior or polluted petrol into our motor cars for we know that they would not run properly in such circumstances. Yet we often put polluted or inferior fuel into our bodies and misname it food.

What we eat affects us not only physically but mentally also. We already know that people who suffer with migraine should avoid oranges, cheese and chocolate, and if one has a cold the avoidance of mucus forming dairy products is most important. Likewise there is a veritable mountain of *foods'* that can, and do cause serious health problems. If not for everyone, then certainly for some. It is no accident that a phrase like *'One man's meat is another man's poison,'* has been passed down through the ages.

'What we think and what we eat – combined together — make us what we are, physically and mentally. '

Edgar Cayce

ARTHRITIS AND GLUCOSAMINE

Glucosamine sulphate is a natural product which has earned a reputation as an effective osteo - arthritis remedy.

It is a major and basic building block of a complex group of proteins called 'glycosaminoglycans' that form an important part of the structure of healthy cartilage, tendons and ligaments.

As we get older, the connective tissue between our joints (articular cartilage) gradually degenerates through wear and tear. It is said that about 60% of the over 60's are affected, often with pain and stiffness in the hips, knees, spine and other parts of the body.

Glucosamine sulphate is often combined with a substance called Chondroitin sulphate which is formed naturally in the cartilage and is believed to be helpful in maintaining its resilience and resistance to damage.

Glucosamine can be found in health shops or may be bought by mail order (which is generally a much cheaper source of supply).

Some arthritis sufferers have found it helpful to cut out from their diet - tomatoes, aubergines, peppers and potatoes - all are members of the nightshade family. Similarly some have found benefit from avoiding citrus fruits, dairy foods, coffee and possibly wheat.

Margaret Hills, a nurse who suffered very severely from both rheumatoid and osteo arthritis, (she had great pain and could hardly walk) on being told by doctors that she would eventually be in a wheelchair, decided that if indeed she were to avoid such a prognosis, she had to become her own physician and find ways to improve her health.

In helping herself in this manner she has been instrumental in helping hundreds of other sufferers by advising them on the elimination of foods which she says build up uric acid in the body.

She also strongly advises that sufferers take cider vinegar (1 dessert spoon of cider vinegar in a glass of water with 1 teaspoonful of honey, three times a day), as a way to combat the disease.

She has written a most informative book called *'Curing Arthritis The Drug-Free Way'* - published by Thorsons.

'He alone is great who turns the voice of the wind into a song made sweeter by his own loving'

Kahil Gibran

* * * *

'When I feed the hungry, forgive an insult and love my enemy – these are great virtues. But what if I should discover that the poorest of beggars and most impudent of offenders are all within me, and that I stand in need of the alms if my own kindness, that I myself am the enemy who must be loved - what then?

Carl Jung

* * * *

'I am committed to a nuclear-free world — the twentieth century must be seen as a century of warning, a call to mankind for the necessity of developing a new consciousness and new ways of living and acting. '

Mikhail Gorbachov

A REMEDY FOR COLDS AND VIRUSES ...

My doctor - Dr Lahkani - told me of the 'sweets' his mother used to make in India to give to her children to keep them free from infection. Using a pestle and mortar, she ground together the following:-

Fresh ginger or ginger in syrup

Lemon juice

Honey

Garlic cloves

She made them into little sweets which lasted some months.

Recently when I was in the midst of a cold virus, I was given a similar remedy by Irma Gomez who comes from El Salvador. She told me to eat a clove of garlic (I could only tolerate this by cutting it into tiny pieces and sandwiching it in a thin slice of bread!) followed by drinking boiled water into which lemon juice, grated ginger and honey had been added. She suggested I take it three times daily but I only took it once a day before going to bed. And it worked!

Thank you Irma!

I find the best honey is Manuka Honey which comes from New Zealand, and apparently is sourced from New Zealand's remote pollution free forests and is world renowned for its unique healing properties. It is very expensive but very, very good.

* * * *

'You already have the precious mixture that will make you well. Use it.'

Rumi

44

O GIVE ME ANIMALS EVERY TME

Oh give me animals every time.
They don't grumble, they don't judge, or lay down the law
They don't shout, or argue, or push, or shove
They just like you, and love you, and hold up a paw.

Oh give me animals every time.
They don't reject you, neglect you, nor do they bore
Or make you feel sad or make you feel bad
And you can always put them outside the door!

THE ELEPHANT

The elephant is an awesome creature
In any landscape, the biggest feature
With impressive body, feet and head
Yet soft and gentle, is his tread.

He is an example to us all,
Loving to his fellows and loyal
He does not kill for sport or pride
But eats the leaves Nature provides.

I've looked an elephant in the eye
And what I saw made me want to cry
Such an innocence and sweetness there to see
So simple, yet so great a creature is he.

SUGGESTIONS FOR FEELING GOOD - WHEN YOU ARE DOWN!
(Not All at the same time! Pick what is right for you)

1. Drink lots of water, filtered or natural mineral.
2. Have someone massage your feet gently with lavender or neroli oil.
3. Have comfort food e.g. porridge, jacket potatoes, chicken soup, toast and honey, banana, boiled egg.
4. Dr Bach Rescue Remedy, four drops in water is very good for stress.
5. Dr Bach Mustard two drops in water can help lift a 'black mood'.
6. Write down all the things you like, or write down all the good things in your life.
7. Try not to get too tired - slow down!
8. Collect quotations that inspire you, write them down in your own book.
9. Tidy a drawer or cupboard.
10. Do a little gardening or go for a walk in the park - not the street.
11. Smile even when you don't feel like it. It can make someone's day.
12. Listen to music - perhaps dance or move to the music.
13. Have your hair done.
14. Vitamin B Complex is good for the nervous system.
15. Stretch your feet and legs. Stretch your arms and spine. Hold your head up high - stand tall!
16. Delegate!
17. Meditate!
18. Watch a funny video.
19. Visit a friend or phone a friend.
20. Visualise a colour you like the most. Blue, green, mauve, are relaxing and calming, yellow, orange, red are stimulating and invigorating.
21. Breathe from your abdomen - Regularly take five deep breaths every hour.
22. Buy yourself something - flowers, a magazine, or some little thing - treat yourself, you're worth it.
23. Look in a mirror and say -*1 love you and accept you just the way you are. You are wonderful.*

These suggestions are tried and tested - They work.

I know two men, one of whom is very happy, and one of whom is miserable. The essential difference between them is that one loves the beauty of the world and the other hates the ugliness. *

T Dreier

'Be humble for you are made of earth,
Be noble for you are made of stars.[9]*'*

Serbian Proverb

'So long as you are trying,
So long as you pick yourself up when you fall,
You will succeed.'

Yogananda

1st AUGUST

Early Sunday morning on 1st August.
The air is cool and fresh and fragrant,
It refreshes me.
A new day, a new beginning,
So quiet, so peaceful.
The day seems to hold its breath In quiet expectancy.
Birds singing sweetly,
Soft breezes gently touch my face.
Church bells call in the far distance.

A smell of jasmine, cut grass, honeysuckle,
Dew on the roses,
Cobwebs glow like jewelled diadems.
A magpie chatters,
Wild ducks fly by, necks outstretched,
A joyful sound, so free.
A little Autumnal chill is in the air,
Cherry tree leaves turning red,
I feel blessed by a loving presence
Tender, kindly, divine.

Under the willow tree, the early sun warms me,
I feel enfolded in love and joy
Chico my cat, leaps with life and happiness,
'Chase me, chase me, catch me if you can!'
Everything is growing, flourishing, unfolding
Sunflowers smile at me
And turn their golden faces towards the sun
Thank you, thank you, thank you!

A CLASSICAL ANSWER TO PAIN RELIEF?

In the biggest research study of its kind, doctors have discovered that listening to music eases the most severe postoperative pain, as well as reducing levels of anxiety and stress.

When music was combined with specially designed jaw- relaxing exercise, the pain was even more dramatically reduced in patients who had just undergone major stomach surgery.

The team which carried out the research on more than 500 patients, says that doctors should advise patients to use music as well as conventional drugs to combat pain. They say it will hasten recovery and reduce the amount of opiate drugs needed, some of which have side effects.

Other research shows that Mozart is the most effective.

At Hereford General Hospital, consultant anaesthetist Dr John Balance is already using Mozart flute music in the operating theatre as a way of distracting patients undergoing operation. It has long been known that music has a relaxing effect and it has been used in several psychologically-based therapies for dealing with stress, anxiety and insomnia, as well as for children with speech difficulties and cerebral palsy. There is also a theory that the acoustics and resonance produced by low-frequency notes in some music may have a beneficial effect on people with rheumatoid arthritis or lung problems.

Although music is known to decrease anxiety, lower muscle tension and distract attention from pain, just how it does all that is still not clear despite years of research. One theory is
that the brain and in particular the prefrontal cortex, is alerted to the sound of music, and in this way diverts some of the brain's attention away from the pain signals.

The soothing effects of music also helps relaxation, which in turn stimulates another part of the brain, the hypothalamus. Relaxation directs the mind to concentrate on relaxing muscle, breathing evenly and reducing thoughts. For many years dentists have been offering patients music, transmitted through headphones, as a means to overcome their fear of dental surgery, relax jaw muscles, and alleviate anxiety and stress.

* * * *

'We who lived in concentration camps, remember the men who walked through the huts comforting others, giving away their last piece of bread.
They may have been few in number, but they offer sufficient proof that everything can be taken away from a man but one thing; the last of the human freedoms - to choose one's attitude in any given set of circumstances, to choose one's own way. '

Victor Frankl

MUSIC AS A HEALING THERAPY

Can you imagine a world without music? Through the ages, music has nourished and healed human beings physically, mentally, emotionally and spiritually. The use of music as a healing therapy is not a new phenomenon. We have all read how David, the psalmist and harpist, soothed and lifted the depression and melancholia of King Saul with his beautiful songs and playing.

In Ancient Greece, Plato and Aristotle considered that music was of particular value medically for people suffering from emotional illness. They are considered the forerunners of music therapy, which is the controlled use of music to heal on all levels. Apollo was the god of music as well as of medicine.

The music of the early church was meant to put the faithful in a receptive and spiritual mood. Music is used today for this purpose in all religions; in Judaism in the songs sung in the synagogue, in the call of prayer for Moslems, and so on.

Music and sound is and always has been a powerful influence in our lives whether we are aware of it or not. Even in the womb we are responsive to sounds, and as babies we may be soothed by our mother's lullabies. Later on, all kinds of music and sounds surround us and affect us. Some are beneficial, some not, for we are (unfortunately I guess) not bom with ear lids that we can close at will to block out sounds that annoy us or that we don't want to hear. A simple muscle test (AK) can show whether the music and sounds we hear strengthen or weaken us, for we not only hear with our ears but with every cell in our bodies. Sounds such as the sea, birds singing, leaves rustling in the breeze and familiar music that we love (I personally like Mozart, Bach and Vivaldi but it can be any classical music) are very beneficial and make us feel good.

Harsh loud sounds and music can weaken us and effect us on all levels; heavy rock music, a loud grating voice, road drills, music played very loudly in hairdressers, stores and restaurants. Even though I may add, that young people love the sounds of pop music and the feeling of being together with their peers.

Some years ago I met a Dr Peter Guy Manners who had invented a machine to show that sound could heal. He maintained that every human being had their own unique sound, their own vibration, and that illness or disease could result if it went out of balance and vice versa. He said that this could be righted by the machine. I was able to witness the freeing from pain of a lady suffering from a painful frozen shoulder (this is considered by doctors as a very difficult condition to treat).

After being on Dr Manners' machine for a short time her pain had gone. Music, as well as benefiting us physically, has a profound effect on us emotionally. It can move us to tears, change sadness to joy, soothe us, excite us and so on.

We can run the gamut of all emotions. We have all heard how bagpipes or drums and bugles in battles were used to stir the soldiers to fight, and the war dances of some African tribes would bring them to a frenzy.

It is said that shell shocked soldiers in the last war were able to recover by listening to Beethoven's music.

So music can excite, and music can calm; it is very powerful. As Joseph Addison said (in Song for St Cecilia's Day):
'Music, the greatest good that mortals know And all of heaven we have below.'
And William Congreve:
'Music has charms to soothe a savage beast To soften rocks or bend a knotted oak.'

Music therapy is used to great effect with autistic children who live in a world of their own and do not easily communicate with others, for music is a form of communication. It is also highly beneficial for children suffering from brain damage, cerebral palsy, the effects of polio, muscular dystrophy and so on.
The music therapist will help and allow them to make simple, spontaneous basic music, perhaps using drums, cymbals, pipes, bells, the xylophone, piano, violin and guitar. Equally as important as the music is the relationship between the child and therapist. There has to be a secure relationship of trust so that the child can feel secure. They can then make music together and feel free to improvise, starting in a *basic* way and gradually becoming more expressive. It is rather like a mother and child relationship where one listens, and one expresses, and vice versa.

In Britain, the Department of Science and Education states that *'the value of music in the personal development and social experience of handicapped children cannot be overrated.'* Music therapy in this way is of course of great benefit to blind children, and deaf children can enjoy music through rhythm, vibration and dance. Singing also, of course, can be a great joy and very healing. It is also considered good for respiratory, cardiac and digestive function. Children or adults singing together can have a very enjoyable time.

Where adults are concerned, music therapy can help the lonely and the physically and mentally sick, to help free them from their feeling of isolation. In the USA a voluntary organisation exists called 'Recording for Recovery' providing cassettes for lonely, physically and mentally ill people. In some hospitals in the USA, music is now played to terminally ill patients, and of course many healers and healing centres in the UK play appropriately calming music while healing is going on.

In the UK the British Society for music therapy was founded in 1958 by Juliette Alvin ... It offers a post graduate diploma in music therapy, as do the Roehampton Institute for Higher Education and the Nordoff - Robbin Centre. The Association of Professional Music therapists in Great Britain was founded in 1976.

This association can supply lists of therapists who may work privately or with the National Health Service.

You can be your own music therapist, by listening to the music that makes you feel good; really listening, letting it flow through you. It can help you when you feel 'down' make you feel energised, evoke images and memories, allow daydreaming and
the imagination to have a free rein. It can make you want to sing or dance and satisfy your heart, mind and soul.

It can be a truly spiritual experience.

As Aaron Copland, the great American composer, said 'A masterwork awakens in us reactions of a spiritual order that are already in us, only waiting to be aroused.'

Best of all, attending a live concert is a veritable feast for the ear and eye, when you can listen to, and watch an orchestra move like a living tapestry under their conductor.

* * * *

'Keep a green bough within the heart and the singing birds will come. '

Chinese Proverb

* * * *

'He who has access to the fountain does not go to the water pot.'

Leonardo De Vinci

* * * *

'When you reach the heart of life, you shall find beauty in all things.'

Kahil Gibran

HEAVEN... WHAT IS HEAVEN TO YOU?

To me, Heaven would be trees, many, many trees, flowers of all kinds, colourful and fragrant especially roses, lilac and honeysuckle.

Birds would be singing and flying about, singing with joy, hearts throbbing with joy, animals of all kinds, happy and natural and free - lots of cats and dogs and little children full of grace and joy of life.

Hills covered with trees, lakes, rivers and streams, fields of com and sunflowers - many, many sunflowers, their bright faces turned towards the sun and gently swaying in the breeze.

And music! Mozart of course - everywhere - and books and poetry and painting. People walking about freely, gracefully and happily hugging each other with loving faces, all doing the things they enjoy in their own time - writing, painting, playing musical instruments, listening to music, looking after the animals, feeding the birds and just sitting and 'being'.

Healing going on with great gentleness and kindness, no judgement, no criticism, no aggression.

An atmosphere of joy, contentment, peace and love everywhere. Beautiful skies and clouds and sunrises and sunsets, no rushing, no stress.

Villages, homes, beautiful food and clothes - warmth and sunlight - freedom, openness, beauty, truth, *love* and the presence of angels.

But this is Earth as it can be and will be!

'Earth's crammed with Heaven,
And every common bush afire with God But only he who sees takes off his shoes The rest sit round it and pluck blackberries. '

Elizabeth Barratt Browning

L'CHAIM - TO LIFE

Well my dear child
How did you find your time on Earth?
And what did you experience from your birth?
Did you feel love, did you feel joy?
Did you understand you were there to learn and enjoy?

Well dear father
I learned a great deal, often through pain
And tried not to repeat my mistakes again
I learned when I gave love, it came back to me
I learned to express my given creativity.

There were so many things for me to explore
And so much to feel, hear, see and adore
I learned to be in touch with You within me
And found there peace, joy and true reality.

Yes it was an adventure, a wonderful show
So thank you, it was glorious as I'm sure you will know.

* * * *

The best preacher is the heart
The best teacher is time
The best book is the world
The best friend is God. *

The Talmud

MESSAGES FROM THOMAS ...

1. 'Your child chose you as her parent because of the gifts you are capable of offering her. Life did not begin at birth Nor did your relationship with your child. It is likely that you have been here before, and chose to return at this important time You have so much work to do together There are so many things for you to discover You have renewed a partnership that has always existed If you honour it now

    Then all the gifts of the past will return to you.'

2. 'This is the first thing you will say when you open your eyes
And perceive reality for the first time:
'What took me so long?'

    'What is true never moves?
    You are the one who is dancing,
    And the whole world seems to vibrate out of control Hold still and you will understand what needs to happen

    Watch your children when they are sleeping
    This will teach you everything you need to know about Stillness.'

Thomas

Thomas (now 12 years old) is a physically gifted child who lives in a Bulgarian school within a monastery. There he is taught with other children by the monks. They teach the children that love is the only true motivation in the universe and is the foundation and essence of every living being. James F Tyman who wrote the book *'Messages from Thomas'* and *'Raising Psychic Children'* met Thomas who was 10 years old and the other children, and states that these children will some day guide the world into this profound realisation, and these children 'are the final link to creating a world of compassion and peace.'

Thomas is able to transmit inspirational messages by thought to others. These spiritually aware children, and many more, are coming into the world *now* —some already have, called by some 'Indigo' or 'Crystal' children. They are aware that humanity stands at a crossroad - peace and compassion or war and conflict at this time which many call 'The Great Shift'. Have you a crystal or indigo child or grandchild? They have much to teach us.

* * * *

If you want to know how the children are working together to heal the world, watch a flock of migrating geese. They fly together and take turns leading the rest. '

Thomas

* * * *

*'Everything we have to say can be summed up in a few words:- Open, Allow, Surrender, Ask, Watch, Listen, Remember, Be, Love. Anything more would be redundant. ***

Thomas

LET ME BE

Lord, let me be loving
Let me be true
So I can be
Of good use to You.

Let me be merry
Let me be strong
So I can laugh
At the things that go wrong.

Let me be patient
Let me be still
So I can hear Your voice
And know your will.

* * * *

*We are all tiny droplets of Divinity. Don't let us forget it and the power of creative thought. '

'Each man is truly an ambassador of God.'

Sir George Trevelyan

* * * *

'Speak nothing but the truth with your tongue'

Zarathushtra

"It's never too late to have a second childhood!"

IT'S NEVER TOO LATE TO HAVE A SECOND CHILDHOOD

When I first heard these words I thought they were a bit 'trite' and maybe not completely realistic. After all aren't we mature, dignified adults? But now I am a grandma to a delightful little two year old girl, I see it's absolutely true!

I share in the joy on Rachael's face when we put on a cassette of nursery rhymes and as she dances and sings. And - I have to dance and sing too, and to my amazement I can remember the words of the rhymes that I used to sing and teach to my children even though my youngest is now 38 years old.

We walk up the stairs together, but Rachael likes sliding down on her bottom and she insists that I do too! I feel more like a playmate than a grandma. We play in the sandpit together, take her dolly for a ride on her tricycle and play ball in the garden. We watch videos of Winnie the Pooh and Maisie, and I really enjoy these videos, they're so simple and sweet and innocent and quite moral, and so unlike some of the noisy, hyped up cartoons and programmes shown for children on TV.

Every flower every tree, a bird flying, a bee, a butterfly are all new and wonderful to her, and through her eyes I see them anew as the miracles they truly are.

The world becomes such a wonderful place.

At last Rachael is tucked up cosily in her cot with a lullaby and cuddles until the next morning and all is quiet. Then around 7am a little bright smiling face appears above the cot and calls out 'Grandma, grandma!' Another beautiful day begins.

Yes it's truly wonderful to enjoy a second childhood.

* * * *

'Mothers hold their children's hands for just a little while - - but their hearts forever. '

Anon

* * * *

'Teach only love for that is what you are'
'Love is the way I walk in gratitude

Gerald G Jampolsky

* * * *
'A baby is a thing of beauty and a joy for ever '

Mark Twain

WHO ARE WE? - WHAT ARE WE?

We are all like tiny bubbles of light floating in a vast ocean of negativity. All around us and beneath us is the deep murky darkness of hate and anger, fear and greed, corruption, despair and intolerance.

We have been given free will, and we have a choice; either to be submerged and sink beneath the dark waters as many do, or with great effort and consciousness to rise above them like the beautiful lotus flower.

The roots of the lotus are embedded in murky water, but the flower rises and blooms above it and *never* touches the mud.

Buoyed up on the ocean, with hope and trust, we are like little lighthouses - radiant houses of light, little lifesaving vessels, there to warn others of the dangers, to protect those in need, and to give comfort, love and healing to the weary and sick in body, mind and spirit.

With joy, love and peace in our hearts we lift our heads to the brilliant sunlight and sky and give thanks to God for the gift of life.

With gratitude and certainty we know ...

All Will Be Well

This message given to me when I was meditating, was given that all might share.

* * * *
'In that just you, is the greatest hidden treasure of all;
In that you, just you, is fulfilment of every conceivable wish.
In that you is utter happiness, contentment and joy. '

Maharaji

A CHILD'S PRAYER

Dear God,
I know you 're there, but I can't see you or hear you or touch you
or feel you. And dear God, do you really love me?
God's Answer

My beloved child ...

1. You see me
   In the eyes of every loving being.
   When a baby smiles,
   It is me you are seeing.
   I am there in every dawn and sunrise,
   Every sunset and in the starry skies,
   In the mountains, rivers, flowers, trees,
   I am in everything your eyes can see.

2. You can hear me
   In each spoken loving word.
   In beautiful music,
   And in the song of every bird,
   In thunder, rain and waterfall,
   In laughter, song and every newborn's cry.
   You can hear me clearly,
   If you will only try.

3. You touch me
   When you touch another With love and with care,
   For each is your sister, your brother.
   You touch me whatever you touch in this world,
   Whether animal, human, bird or tree,
   And when you go within your heart,
   You are nearer than your breath to me.

4.   You can feel me
       When you feel happy, you feel peace,
       With every breath I give you
       I am there without cease.
       I am always with you,
       I will always love you and care,
       So enjoy this life my child,
       For I am ever there.

* * * *

'The best things are nearest. Breath in your nostrils. Light in your eyes. Flowers at your feet. Duties in your hand. The Path of Right just before you. Then do not grasp at the stars but at Life's plain, common work as it comes, certain that daily duties and daily breath are the sweetest things in life. '

Robert Louis Stevenson

* * * *

'Take time to enjoy things - the beauties of God's creation, the many blessings of life. '

Yogananda

DOLPHINS AND HEALING

Dolphins are popularly noted for grace, intelligence, playfulness and friendliness to man. They have been written about in the works of Aristotle, and Aesop and other early writers.

They have been on Earth for at least 30 million years longer than human beings and their methods of communication are far more advanced than any human language. They have a unique way of communicating across miles of ocean by sounds that seem rather unearthly to us.

Dolphins always seem to be smiling due to the curvature of their mouths, and most of us find them very loveable and enchanting. I was fortunate enough to have the delightful experience of playing with a dolphin in Eilat. Touching him felt rather like touching rubber.

However Dolphins are healers too! They became the subject of scientific studies because of their apparent intelligence. Dr Horace Dobbs has for a number of years, made a study of dolphins and has written books and given talks about them. Maurice and I went to one of his lectures, where Dr Dobbs introduced a man who had suffered from severe depression. He had tried everything he could to combat the problem, all to no avail. Under Dr Dobbs supervision, he was allowed to swim with dolphins. During this time his depression disappeared and it has not returned since, as he told us himself. Dr Dobbs says that dolphins seem able to tune into individual energy fields and enable the body to heal itself. There have been numbers of cases where adults and children have swum with dolphins and received benefit.

I recount the experience of two young children who were helped in this way. The first little boy had lost his power of speech due to illness. After playing and swimming with Dolphins in Florida, he was heard to say 'In' when he was told he must come out of the water. Since then he has managed to speak more words, including 'Mummy' to his parents delight. This happening was widely publicised in newspapers earlier this year with photographs.

The second instance was related to me by Mrs Edwina Sterling who took her son Richard then aged six to a Dolphinarium in Key Largo Florida, where teams of therapists etc., work with each child individually. Richard has suffered from cerebral palsy from birth and finds it very difficult to speak due to nerve damage.

The teams of therapists decide what each individual child needs and what to work upon. In Richard's case they wanted him to be able to say five or six words in a sentence so he was helped to build up words. As a reward for his efforts he was allowed each time to throw a fish to the dolphins. There were nine of them and incidentally they were free to swim out to sea when they wished to. Richard had sessions every morning and afternoon for a week and at the end of each session went riding (with supervision) on a dolphin's back. At the end of that week he was able to say 7n *the water with Al.'* I should say that the joy, playfulness and friendliness shown by the dolphins communicates to anyone who comes in contact with them. There are stories (true) of dolphins rescuing people in danger of drowning, keeping sharks away, helping people in difficulties in boats and so on. They certainly are wonderful creatures and we can learn much from them.

* * * *

'We shall never know all the good that a simple smile can do'

Mother Teresa

ADDITIVES

Many of you are aware that the chemical and colours added to food to enhance the flavour and make it appear more attractive can have an adverse affect on our health. This is particularly in the case of children.

Now, various studies have clearly shown that removing the preservatives, colours and additives in food given to children have improved behaviour, sleep patterns and hyperactivity.

One school which banned 27 colourings from its menu, discovered that the children were able to concentrate and behave better, and parents who supported the school by keeping home meals additive free, endorsed these findings.

Other schools have now implemented a full time ban on colourings, etc. and found the children to be calmer and less argumentative. A study for the Food Commissioner in October 2002 found 'the additives used in hundreds of children's food and drinks can cause temper tantrums and disruptive behaviour.'

Colourings in some products (Have you seen the ingredients and E numbers in sweets?) could spark behaviour changes in up to a quarter of toddlers.

This Government funded study looked at 227 three year olds who drank daily fruit juice dosed with artificial colourings and preservatives and found that it had a 'substantial effect' on behaviour. Teachers at a school in St Austell, Cornwall, noticed an improvement in children's behaviour after parents were asked to use an E number free diet for a week.

On this topic, I recall reading about a study undertaken some years ago in the USA with hardened, dangerous, criminals in a prison. They were given a diet eliminating 'junk' food and additives etc., and this had a remarkable effect on the prisoners' behaviour and personalities. They became calmer and easier to manage. Could it be that the 'junk' food being consumed nowadays plus all the additives, chemicals and colourings (E numbers) in our food could be partly responsible for our increasingly aggressive and violent society?

What do you think.

PS. I decided to buy a pack of sweets which are very colourful and have been popular with children for many years. On checking the ingredients (which were clearly stated on the pack in question) and their possible effects, this is what the sweets contained:-

E 171 no adverse effect.

E 104 Quinoline Yellow (can cause hyperactivity)

E 124 Ponceau red colour (should be avoided by asthmatics and people with aspirin sensitivity.

E 110 Sunset Yellow (risk of allergy producing urticaria, swelling of blood vessels, gastric upset and vomiting).

E 122 Carmoisine red colour (can produce adverse reactions in sensitive people or people with aspirin allergy and asthmatics. Can cause urticaria or oedema.

E 133 Brilliant Blue (can cause hyperactivity).

E 120 Cochineal red colour (can cause hyperactivity).

Draw your own conclusion. You can check these findings in the *'E for Additives E Number Guide'* by Maurice Hanssen - publishers Thorsons.

Please look carefully at the sweets you buy for your children/grandchildren.

Another culprit is Tartrazine found in many foods and drinks. It can cause skin rashes, hay fever, breathing problems, blurred vision, purple patches on the skin. Also it may be responsible for wakefulness in small children at night.

However, do remember some E numbers are harmless or at present not known to have adverse effects. You have to be your own detectives!

The Glebe Hall Healing Centre - Stanmore
Through the eyes of a reporter from 'The Harrow Observer'
Thursday February 12, 2004 www.Harrow, *co.uk.*

HEALING HANDS NEEDED TO HELP EASE
SUFFERING
By Liz Nicholls

Love and care is needed now more than ever because of all the suffering in the world, according to a healing organisation which is seeking new members.

Yetta and Maurice Powell of Old Church Lane, belong to the Jewish Association of Spiritual Healers and train new practitioners through a two-year course from their home.

Mrs Powell said: 'We need more healers in the world, especially at the moment with all the violence and suffering. Spiritual hearing is really as simple as breathing and as old as the human race - you see it with mother and child.

Anyone can do it if they are dedicated and it is simply a matter of channelling energy, like turning on a tap.'

Curious newcomers and regulars drop into a healing centre set up by the group in Glebe Road, Stanmore, where trained healers and probationers soothe away cares every Thursday.

Mr Powell said: 'Doctors of yesteryear were more inclined to frown upon complementary therapies like healing when they were less well known.

Now of course, the benefits have been proved by many medical organisations and the two schools of thought marry together.'

The couple, who have been married for 52 years, trained as healers after developing an interest in the subject before joining the association, which has members in the United States and Israel.

Together they edit the group's newsletter and Mrs Powell writes poetry, including a published book called 'Reflections and Rhymes', and she regularly gives talks to bereavement groups from across north west London. She said: 'Spoken kindly, gently and lovingly, words have a reassuring effect, and positive thinking has been proven to strengthen people in body and mind.

Many people who come to us are feeling negative or anxious because of physical pain or stress.

Most will feel the benefit after a few healing sessions and it is their experiences which often lead people to become healers themselves.'

The healing centre in Glebe Hall, Glebe Road, Stanmore, is open to everybody from 2-4pm every Thursday and healing is free, but donations are appreciated. Healers are also available to give information about the process and how to get involved.

Living proof healing works surprisingly well:

Brian Copeland, a heart attack patient said he is amazed by the positive effect healing has had on his health, despite early reservations.

Brian Copeland, 54, of Stonegrove, Edgware, suffered two heart attacks seven years ago and needed a triple bypass operation to clear his clogged arteries.

He became interested in healing in 1997, and after being impressed with its soothing qualities, he trained and went off to become a fully qualified practitioner with the Jewish Association of Spiritual Healers in 2000. He said: 'If you had asked me a few years ago I would have laughed my head off as I thought it was all a load of rubbish.

When I went to see my heart specialist at the Royal Free Hospital, he was stunned.

I should be dead by now, really.

He couldn't understand why the rate of deterioration had slowed and slowed and the explanation we came up with was that I was having healing at the same time.'

Mr Copeland believes the power of positive thinking and energy has the potential to help anyone who is willing to give it a try, regardless of their beliefs.

Although he is a member of the association, he said he does not belong to any religion, but considers faith a personal matter.

He said: 'Healing is a question of channelling energy from the Source, whatever you believe that Source to be, but I don't think you need to call yourself a member of any organised religion to pass on good thoughts and prayers to others.'

This article is taken from the February 12ᵗʰ 2004 issue of 'The Harrow Observer'

* * * *

'Strange is our situation here on Earth. Each of us comes for a short visit, not knowing why, yet seeming to have a divine purpose. From the standpoint of daily life, however, there is one thing we do know; that man is here for the sake of other men, for the countless unknown souls with whose fate we are connected by a bond of sympathy. Many times a day I realise how earnestly I must exert myself to give in return as much as I am still receiving.'

Albert Einstein

UP AND DOWN STAIRS ...

I heard such a lovely idea while listening to the radio. I only caught the tail end of an interview with Pamela Stephenson, wife of Billy Connolly.

I'm sure she won't mind us copying her wonderful idea.

She said that every time she goes up the stairs, she stops on every stair and says a little 'thank you', a prayer of gratitude.

For example, she, stops on the first stair and might say 'thank you for a lovely day' on the second stair, 'thank you for my breath (food, life, etc.) and so on.

Coming down the stairs, she lets go of any problems all the way down.

It's certainly worth copying.

* * * *

*It matters not who you love, when you love, why you love, where you love, or how you love. It matters only that you love. ***

John Lennon

* * * *

'Every kindly smile, every kindly thought and action; every deed done for love or sympathy or compassion of others proves that there is something greater within us than that we see.'

Edward Bach

ONIONS

We are all like onions
With layers and layers and layers and layers
Some onions are bigger
And some layers are tougher
But they all have to be peeled away
Until nothing is left but the essence
It's a bit painful when layers are stripped away
But it has to be.

A baby is like a little spring onion
No layers, just sweetness and tenderness.
Then, the layers start to grow.
We have to protect ourselves
Make our defences against the world
Parents, teachers, happenings, plaster layers on us.
Until as time goes by -
We become tough old onions
With lots of layers
And papery brown skin.

When I peel an onion it makes me cry,
And when I get peeled, I feel like crying too
But it's not all painful,
Because under all the layers
And layers and layers and layers and layers
Is the real true me, the real sweet you.

Teddy the Healer

TEDDY THE HEALER

Do you reader, like me have a passion for teddy bears? Do you possess one of your own? No, not your children's or grandchildren's but yours! Your very own!

I'm not ashamed to admit that I have several - a few little bears reside on a shelf above my bed, a jolly larger bear sporting a red sweater sits on my bed and sometimes in it, and then I have an even larger teddy bear in my living room. I couldn't resist his cuddly soft fur and cheerful face. Visitors are always attracted to him.

Now what has this to do with healing, you may ask? Well in my opinion teddy bears are very healing. We all like to touch them, to hug and cuddle them — they are, I think very comforting. Who can resist them?

I was lucky enough this year to see again the adorable koala bears at the Lone Pine Sanctuary near Brisbane, Australia, and privileged to hold one. They really cling to you, but although they look like real true teddy bears, their fur is not soft but quite hard, almost prickly.

Our daughter was given a very large 2 ft high teddy bear when she was tiny, by a friend called Mike Bulger who sadly is no longer with us. So the bear was called Bulger bear and it had a deep growl when its tummy was pressed. Now he sits on a chair in our porch, wearing a fur (nylon) hat which Maurice bought in St Petersburg which was later discovered to be too small. In the winter we dress him in a scarf and gloves. He's a bit worn now and is minus his growl and one of his legs is all but dislocated. But all are still enchanted by him.

We gave Rachael, our granddaughter, now three, her first bear - a large Winnie the Pooh. I fell in love with him in New York and had to buy him long before Rachael was born. He or she is her favourite and she calls him/her Amy. She has several other teddy bears that she takes to bed, especially her little 'night' bear which goes everywhere with her including Australia. We were very thankful that it came back with her - otherwise I don't know what would have happened! Of course he has to come too when she visits us.

Teddy bears are so comforting and good to cuddle when one is feeling a bit low or lonely. They don't criticise or judge and can be talked to and share your troubles.

I believe that every child (and every adult!) should have a teddy bear to love.

The Freemasons' Provincial Grand Lodge of Essex realise this and they have set up a Samaritan fund which buys teddy bears, which they distribute to trauma units and emergency services so that these teddy bears may comfort traumatised children - maybe a car accident when parents have been injured too. It has been discovered that they make a huge difference.

'Dear Lord
So far today
I'm doing alright
I have not gossiped
Lost my temper,
Been greedy, grumpy, nasty, selfish
Or over indulgent.

However
I'm getting out of bed in a few minutes
And I will need
A lot more help
After that. '
Amen.

Author Unknown.

YOGA...

I first attended a yoga class (Hatha Yoga) many years ago when yoga had not yet become so popular in the West and there were few classes. I was lucky enough to find a wonderful teacher, who although in her late sixties was in sparkling and vital health and enthused us with her enthusiasm.

I soon discovered how beneficial yoga is: physically, mentally and spiritually and I have persuaded many people to try yoga for themselves. My daughter Sharon who is expecting her second child any day now, goes to a weekly class as does her daughter Rachael who is nearly five years old.

Rachael proudly shows me the yoga 'positions' and obviously loves it. As she told me, 'First of all Mummy goes to the 'preganant' and then it's the children's class.'

I am sure many of us have benefited from yoga and as an ex-teacher I truly wish it was taught in schools rather than the physical education they have now. It's much more balanced, flexible and has a calming effect.

First a quote:

'Yoga is a life of self-discipline, yoga balances, harmonises, purifies and strengthens the body, mind and soul. It shows the way to perfect health, perfect mind control and perfect peace with one's own self, the world, nature and God.'
Swami Vishnu Devananda

The Five Yoga Principles are:
1.   Proper Breathing
2.   Proper relaxation
3.   Proper exercise
4.   Positive thinking and meditation
5.   Proper diet.

MIND AND HEART

My mind said 'No!'
My heart said 'Go!'
My mind said 'Let's see'
My heart said 'I need to be free'
My mind said 'It's a ploy'
My heart said 'Just enjoy'
My mind said 'Are you sure?'
My heart said 'It will endure'
My mind said 'Yes - but -'
My heart said 'I'll not stay in that rut'
My mind said 'My problems bring me low'
My heart said 'They will always come and go'
My mind said 'I have other things to do'
My heart said 'I only want what's true'
My mind said 'It's unreal'
My heart said 'Reality is what you feel'
My mind said 'I just don't understand'
My heart said 'You never will, it's a wonderland.'

* * * *

'Do not struggle. Go with the flow of things, and you will find yourself at one with the mysterious unity of the universe. '

Chuang Tzu

* * * *

'The snow goose need not bathe to make itself white. Neither need you do anything but be yourself. '

Lao Tse

NO!

When will I learn to say
No, no, no, no!
When someone cries 'Help!'
I get up and go.

'I need you!' they say
With despair on their face
But I need me *too*
And I need my own space.

I'll help all I can
But you must see
That I haven't got
Infinite energy.

I have things to do
And I need time to grow
So please don't be upset
If I have to say 'No'

* * * *

*The more faithfully you listen to the voice within you, the better
you hear what is sounding outside of you. '*

Dag Hamnmarskyold

* * * *

'Change your thoughts and you change your world'

Norman Vincent Peale

CHILDREN'S HEALTH

Some time ago in one of the JASH newsletters I wrote about some of the harmful colours and additives that are present in many foods and children's sweets. Many are advertised freely on TV and sold in shops, appealing particularly to children with their bright colours and sweetness.

Now at last it seems that scientific research has finally confirmed what every aware parents knows: that chemical artificial colours, preservatives and flavourings are the cause of behavioural problems in children and some aspects of poor physical health. These range from hyperactivity, ADHD (Attention Deficit Hyperactivity Disorder), rhinitis, urticaria, difficulty in sleeping, eczema and asthma.

Fizzy drinks, fishfingers, some tinned food, biscuits and cakes and even yoghurts and children's medicines etc. have been found to be at fault and can be toxic to children's health.

The Food Commission recently found that more than 100 foods and drinks aimed at children, contained harmful additives.

Which raises the question as to how many children have been labelled as 'naughty' or lazy or badly behaved through no fault of their own? How many have been on medication for asthma, ADHD etc?

Unwittingly many children have suffered unnecessarily physically, emotionally and mentally - how many have been referred to counsellors or psychiatrists unnecessarily. What has it done to them?

Read 'Optimum Nutrition For The Mind' by Patrick Holford.

A recent study by Professor Jack Warner clearly showed how additives affected children both in their behaviour and health.

But this was demonstrated many years ago in the USA and there was also a study in the US on hardened criminals in prison. They were given a healthy diet and their personalities changed completely for the better.

So is anything being done about this sorry state of affairs and its affect on our children's health?

The food industry is immensely powerful and it is not in their interests (and profits) to change the food and drinks they produce.

What can be done?

1. Hopefully the Children's Food Bill presented to Parliament by Deborah Shipley MP would, if passed, introduce a ban on advertising food products for children - especially when pop idols like David Beckham and Gary Lineker promote the foods.
2. There should be a *total ban* on all colourings, preservatives, flavourings and additives.
3. School catering should be improved and no vending machines in school.
4. Food with additives should be avoided (read the labels on all products). Only wholesome food should be bought and cooked, the eating of junk food should be discouraged.

* * * *

'Life is not a 'brief candle' It is a splendid torch that I want to make bum as brightly as possible before handing it on to future generations. '

George Bernard Shaw

THE DANGER OF ASPARTAME
As reported on at the recent World Environmental Conference USA

What is it? Aspartame is a sweetener mainly used instead of sugar in tea or coffee, but is now present in over 500 products. (It is often marketed as Nutrasweet, Equal, Spoonful etc.) and is found to a great extent in Diet Coke and Diet Pepsi.

Why is it Dangerous? Because, when the temperature of this sweetener exceeds 86° degrees F, the wood alcohol in aspartame converts to Eformaldehyde and then to formic acid which in turn causes metabolic acidosis. The methanol toxicity mimics among other conditions multiple sclerosis.

What conditions may it cause? Systemic lupus, fibromyalgia symptoms, spasms, shooting pains, numbness in legs, cramps, vertigo, dizziness, headaches, tinnitus, joint pain, depression, anxiety attacks, slurred speech, blurred vision or memory loss and birth defects.

It is especially dangerous for diabetics It deteriorates the neurons of the brain.

Children are especially at risk and should not be given such sweeteners or soda drinks containing aspartame - such as diet coke and similarly sweetened drinks.

An American senator Howard Hetzenbaum wrote a bill that would have warned all of the dangers of aspartame, but it was killed off by the powerful drug and chemical lobbies, 'letting loose the hounds of disease and death on an unsuspecting public'.

Can the symptoms be reversed? Yes, simply by not taking aspartame at all.

Further information on this subject may be found on the internet.

Two doctors will be posting a position paper with some case histories on the deadly effects of Aspartame on the Internet. The doctors are:-

Dr Russell Blayblock and Dr HJ Roberts - a diabetic specialist.

BEWARE OF HYDROGENATED VEGETABLE FAT
(or Trans Fat)

I don't know if like me you roam the supermarket aisles looking in vain for biscuits and other foods without Hydrogenated Vegetable Oil or Fat in the list of ingredients?

Occasionally and thankfully I come across a packet of biscuits or prepared food without this ingredient being listed as being used.

Why do I bother? What is this ingredient and more to the point, why is it to be avoided?

Well there is much evidence that it may be dangerous and hazardous to health.

It is linked to low density lipoprotein (LDL) cholesterol which is bad and associated with the clogging of arteries, heart disease and strokes. Why is it used? Well it improves shelf life of the product, but actually it has no nutritional benefits.

As stated in 'The Daily Mail' by a Consumer Affairs Correspondent, *'this chemical is considered so harmful that US Government experts have declared that there is no safe level of consumption.*

Britain's Food Standards Agency is concerned about trans fat, yet has not warned consumers, unlike the US.

However, it is good to know that Masterfoods Limited, UK, who manufacture Mars, have removed hydrogenated vegetable oil from this product.

It is high time that other manufacturers and food processors followed this example.

Hydrogenated Vegetable Oil is found in many foods such as some cream crackers, some cornflakes, some apple pies and puddings, spreads and biscuits, and unfortunately, many, many other products, including vegetarian dishes and children's foods.

Your health and your family's health is at stake, so read the labels!
'Three things on earth are accounted precious:
Knowledge, grain and friendship. '
A Burmese Proverb.

ARTHRITIS •••

It is said that eight million people in the UK have arthritis. Some people consider that it is part of the ageing process, but some kinds of this disease affect people of all ages and children also. It is the single biggest cause of physical disability in the UK and cause much discomfort, pain, stiffness and fatigue.

There are differing opinions on causes including climate, diet, damage to a joint leading to inflammation etc., and as yet no known cure.

However some help is available. Apart from prescribed drugs and also a natural plant - Devils Claw, and now Glucosamine with Chondroitin, I would like to mention a book which has been very helpful to many sufferers: 'Curing Arthritis the Drug Free Way' by Margaret Hills - published by Sheldon Press.

The author advocates a way of eliminating the pain and suffering of arthritis mainly by correcting one's diet.

Margaret Hills was a nurse and suffered from both rheumatoid arthritis at first and later developed osteo-arthritis. She deteriorated to the extent of having to wear a surgical collar and was told by her doctors that she would eventually be confined to a wheelchair.

With a family of eight children, she refused to accept this grim prospect and determined to find a way to help herself out of her suffering.

In the book she writes how she eliminated all the nightshade family from her diet (potatoes, aubergines, tomatoes, peppers, etc.,) as well as all citrus fruits except for lemons.

Furthermore she drank cider vinegar in water three times a day to eliminate the uric acid from her body (1 tablespoon in a glass of water with honey added if required).

She recommends Epsom salt baths and suggests not sitting still for more than half an hour at a time, but getting up and moving around and then sitting down again.

My dear friend Carol Cobb is a living proof that this advice by Margaret Hills works. Ten years ago, Carol developed a severe form of arthritis. She was in agony, unable to turn over in bed, to walk or go up and downstairs without agonising pain.

I found this book as if 'out of the blue' - synchronicity? - and gave it to her. Carol followed the dietary advice religiously, and within a year all her pain had gone. Since then she has walked and exercised every day and feels fine. She now is able to occasionally have potatoes and tomatoes, but stops eating them if she gets any warning 'twinges'. So I would say that there is a wealth of good information within Margaret Hills' book and is well worth reading if you or any one you know has arthritis.

Five Simple Rules To Be Happy.

1.   *Free your heart fromhatred*
2.   *Free your mind fromworries.*
3.   *Live simply*
4.   *Give more*
5.   *Expect less.*

Anon

* * * *

If you want to be happy, be. '

H D Thoreau

BUTTERFLY

The Butterfly,
Symbol of joy and resurrection,
Is bom as a grab,
And just eats and eats and eats and eats.

And as a Caterpillar,
A crawling, earthbound creature,
Munches on cabbages and mulberry leaves,
Getting fatter, and fatter, and fatter, and fatter
Until his skin splits and bursts, and splits again.

But, he knows the right time to cease,
And spin his fragile cocoon of silk,
And there he will stay in the stillness,
No eating, no movement -
Waiting, waiting -

And in the darkness,
A transformation is taking place,
A miracle of creation,
For from the Cocoon's womb
A movement, a happening -

And a creature emerges
Trembling, delicate
And lifts his antennae to the sky
Wings! - Yes wings!
Tremble and flutter
And open wide and wider.

He rests a while,
And behold!
A creature of great beauty,
Colour translucent, red and blue and gold,
Miraculous rebirth!
And then, like gossamer he flies!
And delicately drinks nectar from a rose.
Grub, Caterpillar, Cocoon, Butterfly -
How did the Grub become the Butterfly?

MORE ABOUT THE HEALING POWER OF
GEMSTONES AND CRYSTALS

Emerald, green in colour, probably the most valuable of precious gems. Known as early as 2000 BC, the emerald was very popular with the ancient Egyptians. It was named as the fourth foundation stone in the wall of the new Jerusalem.

It was said to heal inflammation, used as an antiseptic and considered to be an antidote for poison, as well as healing diseases of the eyes and to improve eyesight, bones and teeth. The emerald is also used as a cure-all, strengthening the heart, liver, kidneys and immune system, improving the memory and toning the body and mind.

It is known as a 'stone of successful love' the jewel of Venus, and is said to promote domestic bliss.

Ruby, red in colour and symbolises contentment.

It is said to be one of the gems used in the breastplate of the ancient High Priest of Israel.

It is thought to encourage gentleness and discourage violence, and was used in the treatment of fever and some heart disorders, and can be used to decrease the length of time for chemicals and toxins to exit the body.

It has been said that as long as one retains a bit of ruby, wealth will never depart and that it protects against unhappiness, distressing dreams and lightning.

Rose Quartz, a delicate soft pink in colour.

The early Chinese used rose quartz for carvings of their Goddess of Peace as the colour was thought to reflect her gentleness and wisdom.

It is said to produce a restful, cooling energy that will restore calmness, balance and clarity to the emotions, and is considered excellent for healing emotional 'wounds'. It may also be used to relieve bums and blisters caused by heat. It is also considered helpful in releasing impurities in the cells of the body and thought to be particularly beneficial to heart and lungs when placed in the appropriate reflex or acupressure/acupuncture points.

Amethyst, colour ranges from deep purple to pale lavender.

The Romans believed this gem prevented drunkenness. It is thought to bestow stability, strength, peace, relieve stress and calm violence and anger.

It is a powerful healing crystal, often used in treating disorders of the nervous system, digestive tract, heart, stomach, skin and teeth. An amethyst placed on the centre of the forehead can relieve the pain of headaches. It has also been helpful in the treatment of blood disease, bums, scalds, infection and oedema.

CRYSTALS

Yes, maybe to you, they are stones,
Or gems to be bought and bartered,
And worn on hand and throat,
But to me, they are shining orbs
Condensed energy of aeons and ages
Translucent and glowing,
Vibrating.

Each is an individual
With its own power and life.
Patterned, coloured and shaped through time
By a Celestial hand
For us to use
Hopefully for good.

NEW YORK, NEW YORK

New York, New York
How could this be!
A city so vibrant
And always so free.

Destruction by fanatics
Who cannot see,
That on this Earth we are all
Just one humanity.

The world weeps for those
lost With heartfelt tears,
For our fellow humans
Their torment and their fears.

We can but send Love and
healing, and pray

That from this hideous horror
Will come a better day.

God gives us the choice
Of darkness or light
Of evil or good
He allows us this right

Though the darkness is strong
And hate's still around
*Remember God's light and love is
all powerful And goodness will*
abound.

Tuesday 11 September 2001, a day etched in our minds. A day of wanton destruction, yet also a day that united the world. A day that poignantly reminds us that all of us are one family and shows us that what hurts one hurts us all!

Let there be solace, peace everlasting, and healing to all those whose lives have been so cruelly shattered and traumatized by these events.

Shalom - Peace

MULTIPLE CHEMICAL SENSITIVITY (MCS)

Have you heard of multiple chemical sensitivity? MCS ... It is one of the fastest growing illnesses in this age, and is brought about by exposure to the many chemicals in our environment that is making many children and adults very ill and unable to live proper lives.

Did you know that there are over 70,000 yes, seventy-thousand chemicals in the environment; in the air, the water, our food (toxic chemicals are added) and in our homes. Carpets, adhesives, plastic, paint, dry cleaning, pesticides, car exhaust emissions, etc. etc. all give off amounts of toxic chemicals. MCS is recognised by countries like America as a disability, and sufferers are helped health wise and financially. But this country appears to be indifferent. Of course it could be said - maybe we are mistaken - that the powerful gigantic drug and chemical companies do not want any government intervention and without doubt the government enjoys huge revenues from these industries. *Profit before health!*

Maurice and I attended the first MCS Conference to be held in the UK to which MPs and MEPs were invited, but not one attended. The speakers were mainly doctors and a video was shown. We saw a young child affected by multi-chemicals. He became terribly ill and nearly died, but fortunately the cause was discovered, the family moved location and the child recovered. We also saw adults originally strong and healthy who had been so severely affected, that they could no longer work, their lives a living hell.

We were also told about the soldiers, marines and airmen affected by the Gulf War Syndrome, some terminally ill with such illnesses as cancer and motor neurone disease, others with asthma, muscle and joint pain, emotional disorders and suchlike. Do you remember as I do, (long ago) biting into an apple which was juicy, sweet and absolutely delicious? Today's apples although they have a good appearance taste like cardboard and are apparently chemically sprayed 17 times!

I have been reading about some of the chemicals that are routinely put into our food and water and it is horrendous!

Can anything be done, or must many more babies, children and vulnerable people suffer in this ever more polluted chemical world? Well there is a world-wide organisation called the 'Campaign for Truth in Medicine' (CTM) 'the force of change' that anyone can join for free and receive regular bulletins and further information . . . Here I quote ... 'It is dedicated to pressing for change in areas of science and medicine, where entrenched scientific ignorance, or vested interests are costing lives.'

* * * *

'Everyone must have two pockets, so that he can reach into the one or the other, according to his needs.
In his right pocket are to be the words 'For my sake was the world created' and in his left I am but dust and ashes. '

Hasidic Saying (Martin Buber)

* * * *

'The enlightened will shine like the brightness of the sky and those who make the masses righteous will shine like the stars for ever and ever.'

Daniel 12.3

YOUR CHOICE...

Now here is an idea for you to think about and hopefully to write about for forthcoming issues of 'News & Views'-

If you were asked who are the eight people you most admire and have found inspirational to you and who you would like to have met and why, who would they be?

You can choose anyone past or present.

Here is my list to start you off:-

1. Mozart - for his sublimely sweet, divinely inspired music, which has been said to be very healing.
2. Leonardo Da Vinci - his paintings, inventions, incredible genius and desire to discover in so many fields.
3. St Francis of Assisi - for his great love of animals, birds and his simplicity.
4. Socrates — He said 'Know thyself — his great wisdom and modesty.
5. King David - for those wonderful psalms.
6. William Blake - mystic, poet and engraver, I love 'Songs of Innocence and Songs of Experience'.
7. Helen Keller - she was such an inspiration to many despite being blind, deaf and mute from early childhood. She graduated with honours in English.
8. Peace Pilgrim - for her love, courage and joy of life - walking 25,000 miles across America to spread the message of peace.

Books recently read and recommended (All worth reading)
'God and the Evolving Universe, The Next Step in Personal Evolution' by James Redfield (author of 'The Celestine Prophecy' and others)

He says 'We believe we are on the brink of a new understanding of who we are as human beings.'

'The Field' by Lynne McTaggart

Bemie Segal says 'A fascinating presentation about the true nature of life.'

'The Reconnection' 'Heal Others Heal Yourself by Dr Eric Pearl - a chiropractor in Los Angeles who discovered that he can manifest miraculous healings.

'Raising Psychic Children' 'Messages from Thomas' by James F Twyman.

Thomas is a Bulgarian boy (then 10 years old) with great psychic gifts, love and compassion.

'Peace Pilgrim and Steps Towards Inner Peace' - the story (by herself) of a remarkable woman who spent the last 28 years of her life on a pilgrimage for peace, walking across America.

* * * *

'This is your chance to be born again. And to be raised in a way that will lead to your Perfect Life.
If you are willing to learn this and give it to the children that are around you now, then give us, and we will give it back to you.
Then you will
remember. '

Thomas

* * * *

'The Lord is my Shepherd
I am his lamb
He loves me exactly as I am.

THE INVINCIBLE HUMAN SPIRIT...

As *healers, we have surely come across people with severe disabilities who have compensated with great courage in some way for their hardships - whether physical, emotional or mental, for the invincible human spirit has the power possibly to overcome practically any situation.*

■ . . With this in mind we invite healers to write about their experiences with patients, so that we can all share them.

If we look at famous people in the past who have inspired us in the way they have surmounted their disabilities and problems, there are so many, but I will choose just a few.

In the world of music, the great composer Beethoven comes to mind. When he realised that he was going deaf (what greater misfortune for a musician and composer) he was desolate and decided he would take his life.

But then after a great inner struggle, with great courage he decided to go on. Out of this victory of the spirit the great 3rd Symphony was born - the Eroica. Sublime music from then on poured out of him although he could not hear it - the symphonies, sonatas, piano and violin concertos etc. At the first performance of the great 9th Symphony - with Schiller's 'Ode to Joy' it is reported that after conducting it, he had to be turned around to see the rapturously applauding audience, because he could not hear them.

Mozart wrote the sweetest, most divine music but was always poor. He died in poverty at 35 and was buried in a pauper's grave.

Vivaldi - the 'red haired priest' whose work has only been recognised in the last 30 years, suffered from severe ill health all his life but produced masses of beautiful music. His 'Four Seasons' are now as familiar as 'God Save The Queen!'

In the world of Art, Renoir suffered from pain racking arthritis in his later years, but kept painting. The paintbrush had to be tied to his arthritic fingers. We all know how Michelangelo painted the Sistine Chapel ceiling lying on his back. It took him seven years and caused him crippling back pain, but the work he produced is a profound experience for the viewer.

In the field of literature and poetry so many poets and writers succumbed in the 19th century to the scourge of the time - consumption, which we now call tuberculosis. Yet in their disease ridden lives they wrote sublime poetry, as for example John Keats who died at 25. William Blake, ridiculed and poor all his life, wrote, illustrated and published poetry and words that are powerful and speak to our hearts. They are so relevant today - simple yet profound. Sir Winston Churchill suffered from bouts of deep depression, 'his black dog', yet he wrote, painted and governed, and his speeches inspired us all. There are so many, many others, names well known and many unknowns - all with a great spirit and soul who fill us with admiration and inspiration for their courage and determination.

Think of that great man of our time Nelson Mandela who despite 27 years imprisonment for his beliefs, remained without bitterness, and with great humility, love and understanding, led and freed his people from bigotry and enslavement. He has become a light and token of goodness and inspiration for all people, especially the young.

I will end with two quotations from Helen Keller who overcame blindness and deafness ...

'Keep your face to the sunshine, and you cannot see the shadow'
and

'Fear, the best way out is through.'

We can all learn from people like these, for life and the world is enriched by them.

* * * *

'It is the lifted face that feels the shining of the sun. '

Browning.

THE GRASS IS ALWAYS GREENER ON THE
OTHER SIDE

On holiday in July this year touring the magnificent Rocky Mountains area in Alberta, Western Canada, we think we discovered the source of the saying 'The grass is always greener on the other side.'

While travelling by coach along a wide two lane motorway with mountains and lakes on either side, our coach driver/guide pointed to bridges at regular mile or so intervals that connected one side of the highway to the other.

He told us that they had been built specially for the wild animals of the region; black bears, brown bears, elks, deer, etc., because when they had eaten - all the grass on their side they saw the green grass on the other side and wanted to enjoy the abundant vegetation there.

Many animals had been killed attempting to cross the road, so the kind Canadians (who protect and nurture their wild life) had originally built tunnels for them under the roadway. However the animals were reluctant to use them, so grass covered bridges were built especially for the animals, and they went happily across to the greener grass on the other side.

* * * *

'One who bears no hatred-who is a compassionate friend to all creatures - who is not possessive or selfish, equal in happiness and distress, and forgiving - This devotee of mine is dear to me. '

From the Bhagavad Gita

SEND BACK A ROSE

If they send you a rock
Send back a rose
For that is how love
Grows and grows.

If they send you a snarl
Send them a smile
It can work wonders
Just try it a while.

If they send you their anger
Send them gentleness
To sweeten the pain
Of their emptiness.

And send them joy
If they are depressed
Tranquillity and peace
If they are stressed.

If they are worried
Show them the sea
It will be there
Long after you and me.

If they are 'strung up'
Show them a cat
With relaxed charm and grace
We can be like that.

If they feel burdened
Show them a bird in flight
And let their problems
Go up to the light.
If they lack self worth
Show them a flower
Giving fragrance and beauty
We too have such power.

If they have lost faith
Show them a babe's eyes
They will see Heaven there
And then realise.

* * * *

'In the end these things matter most
How well did you love?
How fully did you live?
How deeply did you learn to let go?

The Buddha

* * * *

'There are many wonders, but nothing is more wondrous than man.'

Plato

TIME TO CHOOSE

It's time to choose
No compromise
No doubts
No indecision.
Time to choose,
One side or the other.
The chasm is deepening,
The divide is widening
Soon, to cross over
Will be impossible.

Which side will you choose?
Will you choose unconsciousness?
Half asleep, half alive,
Stumbling through life, killing time, surviving,
Uncaring, getting goods and acquisitions
Yet ever more dissatisfied.
Acting without love or moral sense
Life negating
Missing the beauty and true joy of life.

Or will you choose to live consciously,
Fulfilling your true destiny.
Learning, caring, loving
All human life and creatures on this earth.
Valuing the wonder of the gift,
Appreciating the miracle of life
Choosing what you were put on earth for,
Choosing life, choosing God.

REFLECTIONS

Only in a mirror
Can we see our own eyes.
There's no other way
Look deeply and see,
The true being within.
The witness, the friend,
The Lover.

Everyone we meet
Is our mirror.
In them, we see ourselves,
Our hopes, our fears,
Our worries, our faults,
And play out our dramas
On each and every one.

Life itself is our mirror.
Everything is reflected there.
Sometimes it's hard to look
And see the true reflection.
It takes honesty and courage
To keep the glass clear,
And look.

* * * *

*'Man can see his reflection only when he bends down close to it;
and the heart of man too, must lean down to the heart of his
fellow; then it will see itself within his heart. '*

A Jewish Proverb

THE DIVING BELL AND THE BUTTERFLY

This book has been called 'One of the great books of the century (Financial Times).

It is an inspiring and remarkable book about the triumph of the human spirit over adversity.

The author Jean-Dominique Bauby was Editor-in-Chief of Elle Magazine in Paris. At the age of 42 he suffered a massive stroke and on regaining consciousness three weeks later found he was completely paralysed - a quadriplegic, speechless and able to move only one muscle - his left eyelid. He 'dictated' this book signalling with this to indicate each letter of the alphabet presented to him.

Trapped in his body he was unable to move, to eat, or to speak, yet in this book he describes his life in hospital, the food he imagines he would like to eat, his children and events he remembers in the past, all with gentle good humour and without a trace of self pity.

'A book of surpassing beauty, a testament to the freedom and vitality and delight of the human mind.' (Oliver Sacks).

The most remarkable memoir of our time - perhaps any time. '
Cynthia Ozick

'We listen, because what he has to say goes to the core of what it means to be human.' (Robert Me Crum) The Observer.
It is a book that should be read by every healer.

'What comes from the heart, touches the heart. '

Don Sibet

WHY DON'T WE CARE ANYMORE?

Why don't we care anymore?
Why don't we care anymore?
When an old man is mugged and cries 'Help me!'
We're all as busy as can be
When some poor soul falls to the ground
We avert our eyes and walk around.
Yes we close our eyes to another's need
The focus today is on wants and on greed.

Why don't we care anymore?
Why don't we care anymore?
For the suffering of animals who should live free
Defenceless depending on you and on me.
For Third World children starving to death
For the aborted unborn not allowed to take breath
Disease and famine, murderous rage
Does it not merit more than a newspaper page?

Why don't we care anymore?
Why don't we care anymore?
Are we so hardened to blood, violence and war
That we just don't notice it any more?
We turn off that channel on TV
And make another cup of tea
We could care much more for the sick, lonely and lame.

One day, who knows, we could be the same.
So why don't we care anymore?

POETRY

I like a poem to touch my heart or/ and amuse me. I like to feel my heart responding to the emotion that the poet feels just as much as I can with a painting or a piece of music.

Personally I can't just sit down and write a poem. They seem to come out of the blue as it were, at any time of the day or night. I often get a whole poem when I'm meditating which I may forget afterwards. Occasionally I stop and write it down.

Sometimes I get an idea or see a situation which triggers off a poem or a silly rhyme, which really makes me laugh. Hopefully they may amuse others too.

Poetry is becoming more popular apparently, especially in the United States and some well known beautiful poems are being rediscovered. I know when I was at school and in my teens, I fell in love with the Romantic Poets: Keats, Byron and Shelley. Later on I enjoyed Auden, Spender and T S Elliot which was quite a change, and then when I was studying for my degree, I loved Wordsworth and especially Blake and still think they wrote such wonderful poems.

Apparently there is a study going on in the UK initiated by a doctor, who has discovered - as if we didn't already know - that writing poetry is a great therapy for helping people resolve emotional problems and depression. I would say that writing down what you feel is a great way to helping you feel good.

I know that at school we were made to learn poems by heart and at times it seemed such a chore. But now I am grateful, as I can still remember poems such as 'Shall I compare thee to a summer's day' - Shakespeare or 'My heart aches and a drowsy numbness dulls my sense as if of hemlock I had drunk.' - Keats.

I know a lovely old lady who had her 102nd birthday in May. She is very lively and articulate and can recite reams of poetry she learned long ago. I have a book available called 'Reflections and Rhymes' with over 200 of my poems. In my preface I state: 'Poetry is a wonderful therapy, both to read and write. Everyone is a poet as they are also an artist and a healer. The potential is there in everyone. Every child can write poems and paint pictures expressing how he or she feels - and they are often beautiful and moving - until inhibited - often for life by the criticism of a well meaning adult. These poems are not clever or intellectual. They are feelings, expressions and reflections of how we all feel and what we all experience, and also some rhymes to amuse. I hope you enjoy them and will write many of your own. I always carry a notebook and pen and jot down ideas as they come to me (You should try it too).'

* * * *

'Beauty is before me
And beauty is behind me
Above and below me hovers the beautiful.
I am surrounded by it
I am immersed in it
In my youth I am aware of it
*And in old age I shall walk quietly the beautiful trail. ***

Navajo Prayer

* * * *

'At the touch of love, everyone becomes a poet. '

Plato

OUR WORLD

This is the world God has made.
This is the world God has made.
Pure clear water in full measure,
Fresh fragrant air, the greatest treasure.
To warm and refresh us, sun, wind and rain.
Herbs of all kinds to ease our pain.
Fruits, so delicious for all to share.
Other human beings for whom to care.
Animals to comfort us, and help our work hours.
Beautiful scents and hues of so many flowers.
Birds singing sweetly from dawn 'til night
The gifts of body and brain, hearing and sight.

This is the world man has made.
This is the world man has made.
Polluted air not fit to breathe.
Water so poisoned, it begins to seethe.
Sun hidden by smoke and acid rain.
Earth become desert never to grow again.
Medicines to cure that are in vain.
Man killing man - the curse of Cain.
Children starving while food's thrown away.
People in fear of destruction every day.
Animals in cages living only to die,
Fruits sprayed with chemicals by planes in the sky.
Greed and power and lust and hate,
We must learn to care, before it's too late.

* * * *

'Be always with people who inspire you; surround yourself with
people who lift you up.'
                                                    Yogananda

CLONING-

What is your opinion of cloning?

How it is done.

One way is through a process called nuclear transfer. An unfertilised egg is extracted from a female. Then the nucleus which contains the DNA is removed.

A cell such as a skin cell is obtained from the body of the animal to be cloned. The nucleus of this cell contains the owner's genetic blue print. This cell or just its nucleus is inserted into the unfertilised egg which has had its nucleus removed. Then an electric current is passed through it and this fuses the cell with the egg cytoplasm. Now, with its new nucleus the egg divides and grows as if it were fertilised and a clone of the creature from which the cell was taken, begins to develop.

The embryo is now implanted in the womb of a surrogate mother, where if 'all goes well' it will grow to term. Or the embryo can be kept to obtain embryonic stem cells for 'therapeutic cloning'.

Scientists believe that this basic process should work with humans Where to from here?

'The mind... in itself
Can make a heav'n of hell
A hell of heav'n. '

John Milton

HUMAN BEINGS

Shabby poor old man
Shuffling down the street,
Pushing a rusting cart
Battered slippers on his feet.

Grizzled, tired face
Hands so gnarled and worn,
Grubby old cap on head,
Shapeless coat all tom.

What does he think
As he slowly wends his way,
Will he get some food
And perhaps a drink today?

Ragged poor old man
Existing on this Earth.
Once too, he was a baby
Some woman gave him birth.

Did his mother hold him?
Was he her love and joy?
Was his father full of pride
For his son, his boy?

Did he grow to childhood,
Happy and free from care,
Joyful to wake up each day.
What has brought him here?

Spruce smart business man
Striding down the street,
Pinstripes and umbrella,
Well shined shoes on feet.

On his way to daily work
To the great 'rat race',
With warm stomach replete
And bland unsmiling face.

Passing by the old man
Without a second glance.
Does he reflect for a second
That it could be himself by chance?

Passing by each other
They live in worlds apart,
Yet each is a breathing being
With life and a human heart.

All share the same life on this Earth
Whether we're rich or poor.
All share the same way of birth
And leave at the same door.

* * * *

'Who is wise?
The man who can learn something from every man.
Who is strong?
The man who overcomes his passion.
Who is rich?
The man who is content with his fate
Whom do men honour?
The man who honours his fellow men. *

Sayings of the Fathers

* * * *

*Mentally put yourself in the position of others, and then with
the utmost kindness, you will be able to understand and help
them.
There is no greater joy. *

Yogananda

WHAT DOES IT COST? ... IT COSTS NOTHING!

It seems that everything in this world is money orientated. So much depends on money. If you have it you can do so many things, if you haven't seemingly you can't.

But there are so many wonderful things that are free and can make you happy.

Have you ever thought of making your own list? Here are some of mine:-

A baby's smile.

Birds singing - dawn chorus.

The smell of lavender, lilac, honeysuckle, roses.

Looking at trees, Sitting under them.

A letter from a friend.

Someone you love saying 'I love you.'

Kind words and smiles.

Your grandchild calling you grandma, grandpa.

Reading - escapism, humour, inspiration.

Beautiful music - Mozart, Bach, Beethoven, etc.

The sound of water - a river, the sea, a waterfall.

Fresh air in a wood, a forest.

Stroking a cat or dog and their response.

Meditation/Prayer.

Forests, mountains, sunsets, sunrises, stars.

Walking by the sea.

The smell of newly baked bread.

The list is endless!

Here are some 'down to earth' things you can do for free (or nearly free).

Most museums or art galleries.

A walk in the park, country, etc.

Writing a letter. Go to the library and browse.

Window shopping.

Conversation with friends.

Talking to people in shops or at bus stops etc.

Bird watching etc. etc.

RECOMMENDED BOOKS

1. *Man's Eternal Quest* by Paramhansa Yogananda, published by the Self Realisation Fellowship. This is a book I dip into often for its wisdom and its beauty.

2. *Hands on Healing for Pets* by Margaret Coates, published by Rider. 'This unique guide by Britain's leading animal healer shows how you can learn the skill of hands-on healing to help improve your pet's well being and behaviour.'

3. *Ageless Body, Timeless Mind* by Deepak Chopra, published by Rider. A practical alternative to growing old.

4. *The Good Retreat Guide* by Stafford Whiteaker, published by Rider. Over 500 places to find peace and spiritual renewal in Britain, France, Ireland and Spain.

5. *Optimum Nutrition For The Mind* by Patrick Holford, published by Piatkus. 'How you think and feel is directly affected by what you eat.'

6. *The Web of Light* by Diane Cooper, published by Hodder and Stoughton. This is an adventure story with a spiritual message. Diana Cooper states that if you open up to the higher mystical truths that are revealed, your spiritual growth will be enriched.

* * * *

'The greatest blessing we have is that one breath comes in and one breath goes out. No one can possibly be wealthier than this. It is the most valuable thing, even more precious than diamonds. You can buy houses, land, cars with diamonds. But you cannot buy breath with diamonds.[9]

Maharaji

THE CREATOR CREATES

The Creator creates,
The believer believes,
Peace is the want of all men,
But only those who believe that this realisation
Is the ultimate
Will find this wanted Peace.

Trust Him, for he will show you,
All other things are immaterial,
They never last, but, this will last forever.
Your body is but a shell,
But this shell must be kept from harm,
For inside this shell there is something that must be loved,
From this love, comes love for others,
This love is life, happiness and *Peace*.
Written by Sharon Powell At age 15.

* * * *

*True happiness is in the love-stream that springs from one's
soul, and the man who will allow this stream to flow
continuously in all conditions of life, in all situations, however
difficult, will have a happiness that truly belongs to him. '*

Sufi Inayat Khan

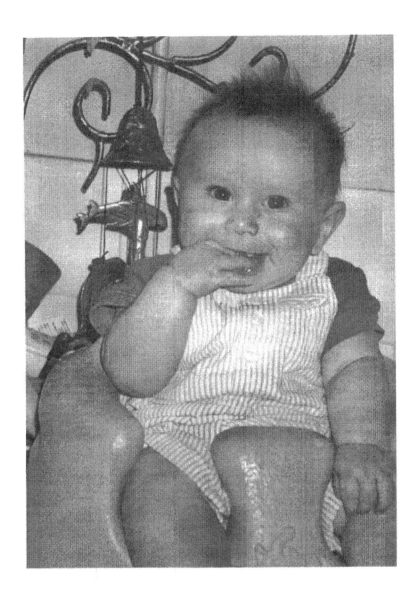

ELLIOT

You smiled at me And I fell in love As your blue eyes Looked into mine.

To see your joy
And your love of life
Is a gift to me
So divine

You really are so gorgeous
And now it can be told
That it truly is so wonderful
For you're only five months old.

* * * *

A child*s hand in yours — what tenderness and power it arouses. You are instantly the very touchstone of wisdom and strength. '

Marjorie Holmes

* * * *

[4] *When you allow yourself really to fall in love with the world, you whole being becomes full of a mother's passion to protect her children and a father's hunger to see them safe and strong.*

Indian Chief

HAPPY GAS

I dreamt that bombs were falling all around
Exploding in the air and on the ground
But nobody got hurt or blown in half
To my surprise, no cries, no, only laughs
For, in every bomb, no mechanism was inside
But filled instead with a heavy nitrous oxide
Not hydrogen or atomic, but laughing gas.
As people streamed into the streets en masse
And as the substance hit the ground and dust
Just everyone started laughing fit to bust
They laughed and laughed, 'til it became a roar
And all felt happier than they ever did before.

The laughter grew and grew, 'twas heaven, sent
'Til it even reached the home of Parliament.
The ministers were talking in despair
Of war, and threats, and violence everywhere,
When the gas penetrated even this solemn hall
And MPs started on the floor to fall
And roll about and clutch their sides with mirth
And gasp 'Oh what a funny, lovely Earth
Who wants to talk such nonsense?
Let's be merry
Let's dance and laugh and sing, be happy - very!'
And even in the Lords, those persons proud
Just lost their dignity and laughed so loud.

In all the prisons, doors were opened wide
Convicts and warders, dancing jigs could be espied
And in the hospitals, as the gas reached the nostrils
Doctors and patients threw away their pills.
Smiling specialists did cartwheels round the beds
And giggling geriatrics stood upon their heads.
The gas in my dream, fell upon the USA
Where people were waking up to yet another day
Of mugging, violence, gloom and threats of war

And wondering was it really worth waking up for
And then the happy gas spread throughout the land
And all grew happy and yelled 'Ain't life grand!'

The mugger hugged his victim, dropped his gun
They laughed together, together saw the fun
The shops, the schools, the trains and all the places
Were filled with merriment and such happy faces.
And to all terrorists the heavenly gas drifted
And instantly all thought of mayhem lifted
And round the world for miles and miles and miles,
Humanity was rolling in the aisles
Prime Ministers and Presidents gurgled 'Let's be friends
No more talks and treaties, now let's make amends
Let's just be friendly, come now, make it snappy
Hooray! The world's gone mad, we feel so happy!'
And then - I woke up -!

* * * *

'Man does not live by bread alone.
He has to handle some hot potatoes,
know his onions, and be worth his salt.
Little wonder man is in a stew. '

Gill Stem

DEALING WITH STRESS

95% of the things you worry about never happen - so deal with stress this way. ..

1.   Just say *no!*
2.   Take a break
3.   Simplify your life
4.   Don't make judgements of others or yourself
5.   Remove yourself from the situation.

* * * *

'Stress is the non-specific reaction of the body to any demand placed upon it.
Stress is cumulative, one stressor adding to another until the body can no longer cope, and moves from ease to dis-ease. *

Hans Seley

* * * *

'Find joy within and express it in your face.
When you do that, wherever you go a little smile will surcharge everyone with your divine magnetism.
Everybody will be happy!

Parakahansa
Yogananda

AUTUMN

The sad raucous cry of crows
Herald Autumn.
A soft, chill mistiness
At early morning.
Dry, brown, wrinkled leaves
Litter the ground.
Geese flying far away
Honking hauntingly.

Clouds skudding, fleetingly,
Sunshine desultory, shadowy
Evenings closing in,
Flowers fading.
A musty perfume in the air.
A smell of burning wood.
A maturing, a mellowing,
Serenity, surrender, resignation
Autumn.

AUTUMN WONDER

Leaves
Falling, falling, falling
Silently, gently
Slowly, delicately
To the Earth
Falling, floating, fluttering
To a thick, crisp carpet
Of gold and orange and brown and red
Each leaf falls at its due time
Falls, falls, falls
And returns to the Earth
From whence it came.

WHAT WILL YOU DO?

So what will you do
With the rest of your life?
I'll enjoy myself, that's what!
I'll do all the things that I love to do,
And ignore those 'shoulds' and 'must not'

I won't allow anyone to stress me out
Or order me about
If I'm depressed sometimes, well I'll get over it
If I'm angry then I'll jolly well shout.
I'll not bottle up my feelings anymore
To be thought of as nice and such a gentle soul.
No, I'll be myself, even if unpopular.
To be true to myself is my new role.

I'll enjoy each moment of each day
Like a child whose eyes are brand new.
See each leaf and flower, birds and clouds in the sky
With wonder and with awareness I will view!

I'll sit under the Willow in the summer time,
And feel the sunshine filtering through.
Hear the thrilling song of the blackbirds
And enjoy the flowers perfume and hue.

I'll meditate and write and I'll paint and I'll walk,
And stroke my lovely white cat,
Listen to Mozart, Vivaldi and Bach
So what will I do? That is that!

UNIQUE PERFORMANCE

So here we are!
This is the stage
The actors are you and I
Living, breathing, sentient beings
The time is now;
No rehearsals,
No encores,
So enjoy the play
This - is - *it!*

So enjoy the play,
Play the music,
Dance to the rhythm,
Sing the praises,
The glory, the majesty,
Of the producer
The director, the puppeteer.
Live it, love it
Learn it, enjoy it!

It's just a short play,
For there are infinite others to be
Performed,
Many actors, many roles
To come and go.
So enjoy *your* play
You may laugh, you may cry
But feel it, experience it
It will never be performed again
One unique, solo performance.

A TINY PLANET

We live on a tiny planet
Spinning in space
In a vast Universe
Of countless, infinite Galaxies
And numberless planets and stars.
We are tiny and fragile,
And infinitely finite.

Yet we humans
Segregate ourselves
Into groups, into religions,
Each one feeling
Their's is the right one, the only one,
That they will be saved
And all the others condemned to 'Hell'.

How arrogant we are,
As Jews, as Christians,
Moslems, Buddhists and all the others
Too many to count.
Can't we see how the differences
Divide us from each other
Creating discord, hate and war?

We are all human beings
Living from breath to breath
With the same needs and desires
Experiencing the same birth and death.
We have to leam to live together
In harmony and love
On this tiny beautiful planet spinning
In the vastness of space.

RIPPLES

Like a pebble
Dropped in a lake,
If I send out a little love
A little healing,
The ripples will expand
And take it further and further,
I know not where,
And I do not need to know.

'Listen
Take time to listen   to the birds
the waves
the wind

Take time to breathe in the air
the earth
the ocean

Take time to be   to be still
to be silent
to allow God

To fill you up with deep peace and love

Mairead Corrigan-Maguire

BRIGHT FEATHERS

With bright feathers I fly
To the sun, to the sky
Gleaming, incandescent, exultantly,
Freely I fly, wings outstretched in joy.

I sing from my heart,
Throat throbbing, gratefully, a glorious song
Of exhilaration, of the air
Rising swiftly past my wings.

With other birds I fly
Singing of life, of wonder,
Of bliss and freedom,
Air, wind and breath.

I did not know one day
A hunter would find and capture me
To keep my beauty for his own
And hold me pinioned to his breast.

Trembling, fearful, struggling in vain
I lost consciousness,
And when life returned
Found myself in a cage of gold.

A tiny space, bars surrounding me,
In terror I beat my wings and body
Against the cold bright metal,
Vainly to reach the sky again.

In vain I beat and cried
'Til my body bruised and bleeding,
Exhausted I lay on the floor,
Resigned piteously to my fate.

I have food, I have water,
I have warmth, I am safe.
Humans come, to admire me
'How beautiful' they say in wonder.

But still within, I see the sky,
Hear the wild birds singing,
As they fly to the stars
How happy they are.

One day my bird within
Will fly away,
Will soar to the skies
And again I will be free.

* * * *

For the caged bird sings of freedom. '

Maya Angelou

* * * *

' You only need one step in order to enter the Kingdom of God.

Just one step. When you hear a bird, or when you see a star, or

the eyes of a child, you can enter the kingdom of Heaven right

away.'

Thick Nhat Hanh

* * * *

'Inspiration is a flow of thoughts that sparkle with life and vigour
– it lies within everyone's power to be inspired and to inspire. '

Yogananda

WHAT HAPPENED TO INTEGRITY

What happened to integrity
Tell me, has it ceased to be?
Does respect and truth no more exist
With hypocrisy and lies now on the list.

Is theft and violence now the right ticket
When people praise those who get away with it?
And is adultery now the norm
For all and sundry to perform?

And what is now considered Art
Touches the sick mind and not the heart
The Turner Prize is an award
Not for beauty, but for fraud.

Why should innocent thousands suffer and die
Because two leaders created a lie
What sort of world is this we make
For children now, and those yet to awake.

At least the flowers still bloom in Spring
The trees wear green and the birds still sing
So let us hope for a true Renaissance
So future humans will have a chance.

TSUNAMI DEC 26TH 2004

WHAT CAN I DO?

Send thoughts of peace and love, and give
To those many whose world's grown dark as night
It may seem little, but you have the power
To change darkness into true golden light

We have kindness and care and compassion to share
Giving help with sincerity and healing
To ease the horror, the grief and suffering
Our fellow human beings are feeling

Let us hope now that this Planet's millions
Have become more aware, and have begun
To realise that life, so short, is precious
And that on this Earth, we are all ONE!

* * * *

*'When indeed shall we learn that we are all related one to the
other; that we are all members of one body '*

Helen Keller

* * * *

*'We aspire to act with the eyes and heart of compassion
We know the happiness of others is our own happiness
We know that every word, every look, every action, and every
smile, can bring happiness to others'*

Thich Nhat Hanh

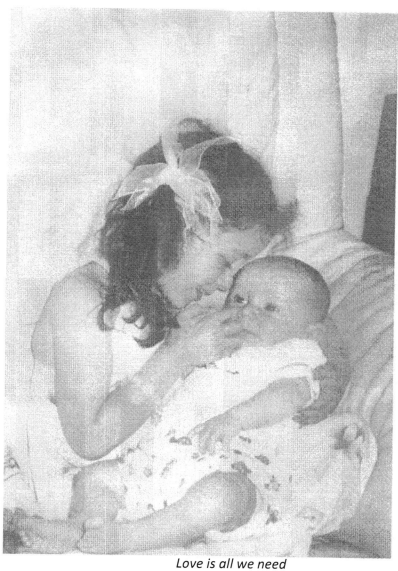

Love is all we need

Printed in Great Britain
by Amazon